Market Domination!

Market Domination!

The Impact of Industry Consolidation on Competition, Innovation, and Consumer Choice

Stephen G. Hannaford

Westport, Connecticut
London

Library of Congress Cataloging-in-Publication Data

Hannaford, Steve.
   Market domination! : the impact of industry consolidation on
competition, innovation, and consumer choice / Stephen G. Hannaford.
    p. cm.
   Includes bibliographical references and index.
   ISBN 978-0-275-99471-6 (alk. paper)
   1. Oligopolies. 2. Competition. 3. Consumption (Economics) I. Title.
   HD2757.3.H36 2007
   338.8'2—dc22   2007016068

British Library Cataloguing in Publication Data is available.

Library of Congress Catalog Card Number: 2007016068
ISBN-13: 978-0-275-99471-6
ISBN-10: 0-275-99471-6

First published in 2007

Praeger Publishers, 88 Post Road West, Westport, CT 06881
An imprint of Greenwood Publishing Group, Inc.
www.praeger.com

Printed in the United States of America

The paper used in this book complies with the
Permanent Paper Standard issued by the National
Information Standards Organization (Z39.48–1984).

10 9 8 7 6 5 4 3 2 1

Contents

Acknowledgments

TERRY FRAZIER encouraged me to begin blogging on oligopolies and helped me through the start-up process. The late Bernie Saffran of Swarthmore College, a rare humanist among economists, was an early sounding board. Various draft chapters of this book were also read by Hanno Kaiser, Steve Schaffran, Rich Henson, Barry C. Lynn, Rachel Hannaford, Fernando L. Alvarez, Dave Pollard, and Terry Frazier. Their feedback was ever welcome, sometimes merciless, and always useful. Above all, I thank my wife, Marion Faber, whose keen eye for awkward writing and fuzzy thinking guided me through the final stages, and whose love, intelligence, and forbearance were my lifelines.

Introduction

ANYONE WHO READS the business section of the newspaper realizes that we are in an age of mergers and acquisitions—2006 set a record of over $4 trillion in deals. Almost every other day a $20 or $30 billion merger is announced. Mere billion dollar deals rarely make the headlines. The companies involved are in every conceivable industry, from gold mining to insurance firms, from ice cream companies to drugmakers.

As if in an enormous game of Pac-Man, many companies now seem to be serial acquirers. Companies like General Electric, Lockheed Martin, and Cisco Systems average more than one takeover a month. They acquire big companies and small ones, domestic and foreign, direct competitors, suppliers, and even customers. In frequent big-fish, small-fish scenarios, the acquirer later ends up being the acquiree.

The value of such deals in 2006 surpassed an earlier record set in 2000 at the height of the dot-com bubble. But the years between 2000 and 2006 have hardly been tranquil, in spite of an economic downturn lasting several years. In fact, over the last fifteen years, there has been an astonishing outbreak of deals around the world, as one famous company after another has been gobbled up, and enterprises dating back to the last century or earlier have been acquired. Look at the small sampling of a vast list of venerable companies acquired over the last few decades that appear in Table I.1. And that's just a small sample. We are in the midst of an astonishing restructuring of the business world that reaches into every industry.

Table I.1. Venerable Companies Swallowed Up

Company	Industry	Country	History Traced To	Acquired By	Year Acquired
National Westminster Bank (NatWest)	Banking	England	Origins go back to 1650	Royal Bank of Scotland	2000
Boots	Retail pharmacy	United Kingdom	1849	Alliance UniChem	2006
Schering	Pharmaceuticals	Germany	1851	Bayer AG	2005
Bethlehem Steel	Steel	United States	1857	International Steel Group, later Mittal	2001, then 2005
Boston Globe	Newspaper	United States	1872	*New York Times*	1993
Paribas	Banking	France	1872	Bank Nationale Populaire	2000
Burroughs Wellcome	Drugs	England	1880	GlaxoSmithKline	2003
Wella	Hair care	Germany	1880	Procter & Gamble	2003
Maytag	Appliances	United States	1893	Whirlpool	2006
Ralston Purina	Animal feeds, pet food	United States	1894	Nestlé	2001
Sears	Retailing	United States	1898	Kmart	2004
Gillette	Razors	United States	1901	Procter & Gamble	2005
Amoco	Oil	United States	1910	British Petroleum	1998
McDonnell Douglas	Airplanes	United States	1921 (merged with McDonnell Aircraft I 1967)	Boeing	1997
Chrysler	Automaking	United States	1925	Daimler Benz	1998
Volvo	Automobiles	Sweden	1926	Ford	1999

Source: Company Web sites.

EVER-BIGGER COMPANIES

All this merger and acquisition activity makes for fewer, bigger companies in each industry. Even in industries that have been traditionally decentralized, such as hospitals, hotels, or commercial printing, the trend to consolidation has been unmistakable.

You can see the changes in many retail categories: what was once a proliferation of local stores has turned into a few big chains that make life hard for the little guys. Small bookstores are dying, the local hardware store is gone, the neighborhood pharmacist has sold out, and the stationery store is a thing of the past. The (independent) butcher and baker are as forgotten as the candlestick maker.

Local chains have been grafted onto regional ones, then onto national ones. And in most high-visibility industries that have always been dominated by big players, that domination has become even more absolute. Coca-Cola and PepsiCo have always been dominant players in the U.S. carbonated soft drink area, but since the mid-1990s, they have diversified into fruit juice, bottled water, and iced tea, while PepsiCo has become (through the acquisition of Frito-Lay) the world's #1 snack company. Big banks and insurance companies have always been around, but the big ones are getting bigger all the time. And the reach of many of these companies has rapidly become global, so that Pizza Hut and KFC are staples of the Japanese landscape, Citigroup and HSBC have offices in virtually every country, and Unilever and Procter & Gamble sell shampoo and detergent around the globe.

So what's so wrong with this picture? Isn't it just the free market doing what it does best? Why should I care how many iron mining companies there are or sneaker makers, as long as they give me what I want? In fact, it is often argued that these companies deserve their preeminence earned through hard work and cleverness, and that the weak sisters have dropped out while the fittest survive. These big companies deliver the riches of the world to our shopping carts and they all speak Visa and MasterCard. As long as they don't abuse their preeminence by jacking up prices excessively, who cares? Isn't that what free-market capitalism is all about?

WHAT THE ECONOMISTS SAY

Economists don't say much. There is a discipline of microeconomics called industrial organization that studies the structure of industries, competition within industries, and company strategies. This discipline also covers the issue of *oligopoly*, the situation where a small number of companies dominate an industry—a situation that is becoming the norm in many industries and is the subject of this book.

But economists have relatively little to say about oligopoly. A surprisingly frank paragraph in a standard college textbook for industrial organization (the discipline that deals with competition) notes the following:

Oligopoly therefore also involves indeterminacy, because it provides a whole range of possible outcomes. Outcomes vary because there are infinite varieties of both oligopoly structures, which differ in concentration, inequality among leaders, and other elements, and attitudes and motives among the leading firms. The shining hope of theorists has been to find deterministic solutions to the slippery, smoke-and-mirrors indeterminacy of the oligopoly problem.[1]

What you can find in the literature is a plethora of articles using game theory to describe the possible outcomes of various competition structures, much as you can explain the strategies and motivations of poker or blackjack players. The authors of the textbook deem the game theory approaches to the oligopoly problem as a failure. "Game theory has not yielded a single model to explain oligopoly."[2]

It's impossible, they conclude, to reduce oligopoly to a mathematical model, no matter how subtle and multivariate the math, because of the sheer number of variables involved. Those game theory models that do exist (Cournot, Bertrand, and Stackelberg) describe a simplified world that only exists in the classroom.

In a similar vein, a widely used college microeconomics textbook admits the basic problem. "The analysis of oligopoly turns out to present some puzzles for which there is no easy solution."[3]

It's understandable that for those who are determined to capture the world in mathematical models, such variability is frustrating, but they ignore the field at their peril. As hard as it is to analyze mathematically, the drive toward oligopoly is one of the biggest factors in the current economy and ignoring its pervasiveness gives a distorted view of what is happening in world markets.

WHY THIS BOOK?

This book is an attempt to make some sense out of the phenomenon of global industrial consolidation. My blog, www.oligopolywatch.com, began with simple curiosity about why company A decides to buy company B, for example, why international food and household products company Unilever bought out "counterculture" icon Ben & Jerry's. I looked in vain for a larger discussion of the issues of business concentration, and I found that the vocabulary for describing what is going on to be less than adequate. Over the years, I have started developing such a vocabulary.

Let me admit that I am no economist nor do I pretend to be. I've worked for years as a business and technology journalist. What I am most interested in is the motivation and behavior of those who run businesses. Behavior is always indeterminate, impossible to express in equations, but there are principles that underlie behavior—patterns that we can see in play. These principles have little predictive value, but they do help to explain why executives and markets act the way they do. Such business decisions are indeterminate, but they are not random, and they can be analyzed and discussed.

For me, it is the variety of possible outcomes that makes the study of oligopoly so fascinating. I hope that this book will contribute to the discussion of this significant trend, one which affects us every time we drink a cup of coffee or watch a TV program. More important, the maneuvers of the biggest companies have a profound impact on our social welfare, political institutions, and global demographics. It's important to have a better way to debate the often-troubling impact of business concentration.

The example and sources I've drawn from in this book are generally the very business pages that got me thinking about oligopolies. These sources, including the *Wall Street Journal, New York Times, Financial Times, BusinessWeek, Fortune, Forbes,* the *Economist,* and CNNmoney.com, focus on mergers and acquisitions when they happen. In themselves, these sources are hardly antibusiness, but they do contain the seeds of a critical analysis of the oligopolizing economy.

Although the facts presented in this book are as verifiable as I can make them, there may be errors on my part that I believe will have little effect on the point of my overall arguments. What's more, any of the specific information about who owns what is likely to have changed because of deals that have taken place since we went to press. Who knows? Maybe Toyota will buy Ford, ExxonMobil split up into two companies, or Tesco buy Kroger. The principles are the focus, and future moves will, I believe, reconfirm them.

THE PRINCIPLES OF INDUSTRY CONSOLIDATION

The principles we present in the book follow. The less familiar terms will be defined in the course of the book. These principles are arranged in the order they occur in the book.

- All industries now tend toward concentration (oligopolies).
- Oligopolies grow from national to global.
- The new oligopoly concentrates in a few business segments, unlike a conglomerate.
- The object is to be #1 or #2 in each field.
- Oligopolies beget oligopsonies and vice versa.
- Only the big can serve the big.
- The sweet spot in business is being both an oligopoly and an oligopsony (an oligonomy).
- Industries tend to form interlocking tiers of oligonomies.
- The growth imperative forces companies to acquire others.
- Big companies need to buy innovation through acquisitions.
- Big companies are motivated as much by fear of disruption as by greed.
- Oligopolies operate more by lowering costs (from labor and suppliers) than by raising prices.
- Big companies are expert at influencing government policy at every level from municipal to global.
- Big companies tend to behave increasingly like their rivals.

1 / *The New Oligopoly*

MONOPOLIES

MOST PEOPLE ARE FAMILIAR with the concept of a monopoly, a situation in which one company or person controls a market by being the single source of some product or service. And pretty much everyone agrees that monopolies are bad in many ways: they eliminate competition in terms of price, quality, service, and variety. Some readers may remember the Lily Tomlin quote: "We don't care. We don't have to. We're the phone company."

But that joke from the 1970s no longer makes the same sense—at least, it didn't until recently. In 1984, the monopolistic phone company, AT&T, was split up after an antitrust action by the U.S. government. It was chopped into a half-dozen regional companies along with a national long-distance company that retained the AT&T name. This was one of the high watermarks of American antitrust regulation, as it introduced real competition into an area that looked to be a perpetual monopoly hosted by one of the world's most powerful companies. The phone industry has since swung back from fragmentation to the current wave of concentration, but there is no longer a monopoly.

And that's typical. Except in rare cases, monopolies don't exist in major industrialized countries. Competition in a free market is the watchword of modern capitalism, and those days when governments or kings granted an individual or group exclusive licenses to sell certain products are long gone. And as free trade and globalism reach into every corner of the world, most of the remaining local monopolies in smaller economies are gradually being eliminated.

Look, for example, at Microsoft. As we write, it's just coming out of a long series of antitrust suits both in the United States and Europe. In the end, for various reasons, the antitrust actions have fizzled out—at least in the United

States[1]—but the lawsuits have certainly cost Microsoft in terms of industry initiative and legal fees, as well as certain restrictions on how it does business. The advantages of standard file formats and applications in the computer industry are, it is generally agreed, offset by the repressive power of having a single company control a market, a situation that hurts other companies and society in general by repressing innovation and price competition. Perhaps even worse, the cost of everyone using Microsoft software has been the growth of software viruses attacking the well-known holes in the Microsoft monoculture.

That kind of market domination by one company, one with more than 80 percent or 90 percent market share of a product or service, is rightly seen as a danger. Only a few public utilities, perhaps water or electricity, can justify having a single provider. These are sometimes called "natural monopolies," since the idea of running two parallel electric grids or municipal water systems is clearly wasteful. But even so, such monopolies are local in nature and highly regulated. Moreover, such older monopolies as the local telephone and the national postal service have been forced to face new competition lately, thanks to cell phones, overnight delivery services, and e-mail.

OLIGOPOLY DEFINED

Monopoly, by and large, is no longer a major issue. But the urge to corner the market is still alive. It now takes the form of *oligopoly*, and oligopoly is becoming the rule in an increasing number of industries.

Oligopolies have been around as long as commerce has. The term, in its narrowest sense, means a market in which there are few sellers of a product or service. Instead of an open market with lots of companies contending for your business, you are faced with a few big companies that, between them, control the entire market.

The existence of oligopolies changes the nature of a free market. While they can't dictate price and product availability as absolutely as a monopoly can, they can make explicit or silent agreements about such matters. Members of an oligopoly might not compete too hard against each other for your business, since it is in all their interests to maintain a stable market and profitable prices. As one standard college economics textbook puts it, "The oligopolists are torn between the desire to outwit competitors and the knowledge that by cooperating with other oligopolists to reduce output, it will earn a portion of the higher industry profits."[2]

In a sense, oligopolies of a sort made up many of the so-called trusts of the late nineteenth and early twentieth centuries in the United States—including Standard Oil, American Tobacco, American Sugar, and U.S. Steel. Careful coordination made oligopolies into *trusts*, something far more akin to monopolies. As trusts, these companies and their (few) competitors openly conspired to hold or drive up prices and to keep out other competitors.

Their predatory nature led to a political reaction in the United States, culminating with the investigative reporting of Ida Tarbell and other muckrakers in

OLIGOPOLY

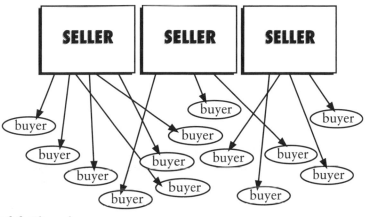

Figure 1.1 Oligopoly.
Artist: Andrew Hoffman

the early 1900s and leading to the gradual (if often reluctant) enforcement of the Sherman Antitrust Act and other antitrust measures. Through a long series of new laws and court cases, the trusts were curbed. Since the 1920s, the threat of cartels, always present, has been kept somewhat at bay because of antitrust policy and economic circumstances. But modern oligopolies have found ways to reach market dominance without forming cartels.

THE MOVE TO CONSOLIDATION

Since the 1990s and through the first decade of the 2000s, an enormous wave of consolidation has been taking place in all kinds of businesses. In more and more industries, there are fewer and fewer companies, whether suppliers of products or services. This wave of mergers and acquisitions has only one parallel, a movement that occurred a century before, during the 1890s and the first decade of the1900s, the era of trusts. But there is one big difference. The oligopolies and cartels of the trusts era were generally limited to the United States. Today's oligopolies are global.

What we have now is something different from the old trusts in another way. It is a pattern of corporate behavior that I will call the *new oligopoly*. This pattern (as well as the principles that underlie it) isn't proclaimed in annual reports, and it is only hinted at in the business press. This new kind of oligopoly underlies many of the actions that take place in every market and grows stronger and more universal every year. Describing the behavior and consequences of the new oligopoly is the object of this book.

The new oligopoly is made up of national or multinational corporations that have chosen specific products or service categories to dominate. In each

A Hundred Years Ago

The headlong consolidation of so many industries of the past ten years has a precedent. In fact, a similar scramble to market domination by a few companies took place a hundred years ago. At that time, business was synonymous with manufacturing. Today's consolidation exists in an even wider spectrum of companies, but the parallels are instructive.

This movement is well documented in *The Great Merger Movement in American Business, 1805–1904*:

> Between 1895 and 1904 a great wave of mergers swept through the manufacturing sector. Nothing like it had ever been seen before, or has been seen since. Although subsequent waves of mergers have occurred, they have typically involved the acquisition of one or more small firms by a large competitor or, more recently, by a firm in a completely different industry. By contrast, in the turn-of-the-century mergers, the predominant process was horizontal consolidation—the simultaneous merger of many or all competitors into a single, grand enterprise.[3]

Of course, things are different this time around. From "single, grand enterprises" (monopolies), we are now seeing a few competitors (oligopolies). But the parallels between 1895–1904 and 1995–2004 are striking. How long-lasting were the roll-ups?

Some mergers led to short-lived domination (American Linseed, American Writing Paper, United States Bobbin & Shuttle). These companies sooner or later went out of business because of disruptive changes in their industries. On the other hand, a number of the firms that were predominant at the turn of the century still are, or have been powerhouses up until a few decades ago: Eastman Kodak, U.S. Steel, International Paper, DuPont, and Pittsburgh Plate Glass (now PPG Corp.). Other companies of the time now form key parts of oligopolies: American Chicle (after many changes in ownership now a part Cadbury Schweppes), Otis Elevator (part of United Technologies), National Biscuit Company (Nabisco, now part of Kraft), and Union Bag & Paper (now part of International Paper).

The history of Continental Tobacco shows both of these consolidation waves at work. It was merged into American Tobacco (1901) to make Consolidated Tobacco, later renamed American Tobacco again. American Tobacco, which ended up owning over 90 percent of the domestic market, was broken up by the U.S. government's antitrust regulators into five companies (1929). These companies were American Tobacco, Liggett & Myers, British American Tobacco (BAT), Lorillard, and R.J. Reynolds, each of which got some of the old company's brands. The new American Tobacco eventually became American Brands. American Brands was sold to BAT in 1994. In 2004, BAT acquired R.J. Reynolds, so now only two big tobacco companies dominate the market.

One other big difference—the market dominators of the early twentieth century were national in scope. Today's new oligopolies generally are global.

category, over time, only two to five major players prosper in an oligopoly, holding a dominant market share between them. It is in all their interests that starting a new company in that market segment should be difficult, and the few new enterprises that do succeed in entering the market are often gobbled up or run out of business by the oligopolies.

EXAMPLES OF NEW OLIGOPOLIES

How common are oligopolies? Let's look at the market in the United States and identify just a few examples:

- Three companies own over 80 percent of the carbonated soft drink industry.
- Three companies sell over 80 percent of the beer.
- Three companies sell over 80 percent of the cigarettes, and two companies sell over 70 percent of the cigars.
- Four companies sell over 80 percent of all the recorded music.
- Four companies own virtually all railroad operations.
- Six companies produce and market over 85 percent of all the movies.
- Two companies own a majority of the radio market.
- Three companies make over 95 percent of all the razors and razor blades.
- Two companies sell over 80 percent of all the cookies and crackers.
- Two companies manufacture and sell over 50 percent of all the toys.
- Two companies sell over 75 percent of all the carpets.
- Four companies sell over 80 percent of all the breakfast cereals.
- Two companies sell over 85 percent of the light bulbs.
- Three companies sell over 90 percent of consumer batteries.
- Three companies sell almost all of the tractors and combines.
- Five companies slaughter and package most of the beef, four companies slaughter and package most of the pork, and three firms slaughter and package virtually all of the poultry (and several companies are leaders in more than one of these areas).

That's just a small sampling.

In many other industries that are not quite oligopolies yet, there is a major roll-up narrated in every day's headlines. While there are around a dozen major banks in the country and hundreds of smaller ones, at least six of the top twelve banks have combined forces in the last few years to make national megabanks. Of a dozen major pharmaceutical companies (themselves the product of repeated mergers) a few years ago, at least three have been swallowed up or merged. Mergers in the U.S. oil industry reduced the ten major players not long ago to five. Similar changes have happened in coal and natural gas, gold, and copper. And any of these numbers may well be obsolete, since multibillion dollar mergers and acquisitions take place almost every day.

Of course, some industries have a much lower level of overall concentration. Traditionally, such industries as sit-down restaurants, funeral homes, and commercial printing companies have been dominated by small, family-run companies. But even that is changing, too, as the trend toward industry concentration reaches throughout the economy.

THE URGE TO CONSOLIDATE

That leads us to the most basic principle of the new oligopoly. In general, *industries tend toward oligopoly.*

There are exceptions to this principle, of course, and we'll discuss them later. But the general tendency is one of the most persistent phenomena of the current economy. We might even call it economic entropy, as the urge to simplify markets has been sanctioned by regulators and by common practice and as the requirements of a global economy make any other course unlikely.

Hasn't this urge to merge always existed? Yes, in a sense. Any business would be glad to knock competitors out of the market, and all corporations have been eager to grow bigger than their rivals. But never before has the desire to create oligopolies been as intense, as methodical, as pervasive, and as global as it is now. Merger activity, as measured in dollars, has increased a hundredfold since the 1980s, with deals worth over $10 and $20 billion common in the last ten years.[4]

OLIGOPOLIES AND CONGLOMERATES

We want to distinguish oligopolies from *conglomerates*. While each company in the new oligopoly tends to concentrate in a small number of core businesses, conglomerates tend to take on a variety of often-unrelated markets. The business orthodoxy, which has changed in the last few decades, is that there should be a sensible reason for moving "horizontally" to take a position in another market.

The problem with expanding randomly is demonstrated in the most famous conglomerates of the 1960s and 1970s. In its time, Gulf+Western was involved in oil, moviemaking (Paramount), television production (Desilu), recording (Stax), rocket engines, tractors (Allis-Chambers), stereo components, finance (Universal American), publishing (Simon and Schuster), auto parts, cigars (Dutch Masters, El Producto), and many more. ITT was similarly diverse: telecommunications (its original business), auto parts (ATE brakes), hotels (Sheraton), gambling (Caesars Gaming), baking (Wonder Bread), vending machines (Canteen), airport parking (APCOA), pumps (Goulds, Flygt), rental cars (Avis), insurance (Hartford), cosmetics, publishing (Sams Technical Publishing), sports (Madison Square Garden), and so on. The company even tried to acquire ABC in 1966.

Both companies crashed and split up in the 1980s, and the wonder is how they lasted as long as they did. Only the ego and energy of their CEOs, one

Japanese Conglomerates

One major relic from the age of conglomerates is that of the largest Japanese corporations. These companies are among the most famous in the world—Sony, Panasonic (Matsushita), Sumitomo, Canon, Mitsubishi, Hitachi, Toshiba, Sharp, and so on. Some are based on banking operations (Mitsubishi, Sumitomo) and are called *keiretsu*, though that term sometimes loosely applies to all Japanese conglomerates.

These companies are involved in a shopping list of diverse enterprises. For example, Sony makes movies; produces and sells recordings; sells televisions, cameras, Walkmen, PlayStations, and computers; and manufactures semiconductors and cell phones. Matsushita makes computer and home entertainment equipment, too, along with semiconductors, kitchen appliances, welding machines, medical equipment, phones, batteries, electrical motors, industrial laminates, and so on. Sumitomo makes sheet glass, tires, chemicals, and (through its NEC subsidiary) electronic products. It also is big in banking, insurance, and coal mining.

It's often been noted that these companies are reluctant to leave any market once they've entered it. That is why digital cameras, laser printers, stereo systems, televisions, and CD media all come from so many competitors that few of them can earn significant market share. Add in the similar Korean companies like Samsung and LG (Goldstar), and you have some very crowded markets.

But even these conglomerates are changing. In the last few years there have been significant mergers, including Kyocera and Mita, as well as Konica and Minolta, Suntory Pharmaceuticals and Dai-Ichi, and Sumitomo and Sakura. Furthermore, control of some companies has been bought by foreign companies (Nissan by France's Renault, Mazda by Ford). This is far more activity than seen in the past, and some key areas are seeing greater concentration.

Big companies are still doing business, and they wield a lot of economic power. But that power has waned in recent years. Even when they have enormous successes in one field (Sony's PlayStation), these successes are offset by losses in other areas (Sony Music). From a competitive point of view, the specialized company with an oligopoly in a few fields appears to be a more successful competitor in general. It is notable that Japan's biggest current success story is the highly focused Toyota automotive company, no conglomerate at all.

---

suspects, kept them together. Their markets were so many and so different in profit models and sales cycles that there was no way they could be properly managed in coordination.

In recent years, we've seen companies that similarly got off target, although in a more modest way. Vivendi (a water utility company), driven by the ambition of its CEO, got into the entertainment industry, disastrously, by buying Universal. Sony went from technology and manufacturing into both music and movies, and both areas have been problem children. Tyco acquired everything from electronics to health care, adhesives to alarm systems, and ended up as another failure, one tinged with fraud. Time-Warner got into the technology business with AOL, and that deal has become a watchword for disastrous diversification.

Richard Branson's Virgin brand, which is used for airlines, cosmetics, soft drinks, electronic games, records, radio, mobile phones, credit cards, and more, looks like the very model of a current-day conglomerate. In fact, most of these enterprises simply license the name from Branson, and the ownership and management of the various enterprises is independent.

General Electric (GE) stands out as one of the few thriving U.S. companies that has a similarly diverse portfolio and that actually does well. GE owns NBC, Universal TV, and film operations (recently acquired from the aforementioned Vivendi), a world-leading finance business, home appliances, aircraft parts, security systems, light bulbs, and so on. The famous quality management philosophy and business cunning of GE CEO Jack Welch were tested to the fullest extent in keeping such a motley collection of businesses straight. And GE seems to be doing well even since Welch retired in 2001. In fact, the company acquires several small to midsize companies every month. Few other companies have the discipline and infrastructure to do it, and even GE is careful to expand only in those six or so areas in which it is already very strong. (Notably, it recently sold off its insurance and silicone materials divisions, in the pursuit of more profitable operations.)

As distinguished from a conglomerate, the pattern of the modern multinational oligopoly (the new oligopoly) has been to acquire in markets that are adjacent to, or parallel to, the ones they already own. Or, alternatively, to buy vertically in other parts of the supply chain in which they already have a presence.

For example, PepsiCo has made a great success with its Frito-Lay snack food branch. It's a similar business to its core beverage line, with pretty much the same set of retailers, similar profits per unit sold, similar delivery and inventory problems, and the same set of consumers to whom they market. On the other hand, Pepsi sold off its ownership of the KFC, Pizza Hut, and Taco Bell restaurant chains in 1997, partly because they had a completely different business model from soft drinks. Pepsi recognized that it became too much like patting your head and rubbing your stomach at the same time.

Similarly, Cadbury Schweppes has been a big player in two markets: beverages and candy, two very similar industries. Clear Channel specializes in radio and billboards. Unilever sells both groceries and personal/home-care products. All of these companies strive to be leaders in each of their fields and being in too many diverse markets would be a distraction to that goal.

Oligopolies, unlike conglomerates, are specialists.

THE EQUITY GROUP EXCEPTION

One exception to this rule of oligopolies, not conglomerates, is the behavior of a growing set of holding companies—that is, the private investment bank or private equity company. These companies include such famous names as the Carlyle Group, Bain Capital, Kohlberg Kravis Roberts (KKR), and so on. These companies, with ever-growing coffers from pension funds and private investors, specialize in acquiring a variety of companies, taking them private, "reengineering" them away from the pressures to keep stockholders happy from quarter to quarter, and then, usually, cashing out with a new stock offering or a sale to another company. This process usually takes between two and five years and often realizes a hefty profit for the equity firm.

There is a contrast between equity buyers and so-called strategic buyers, that is, companies that buy others not as a temporary investment but as a key part of their growth strategies.[5]

These investments are quite diverse. The Carlyle Group, for example, currently owns such business as Texas gas wells, a Korean office building, a U.S. auto parts maker, a Connecticut HMO, and so on. But, typically, these are short-term investments. Take for example, Egencia, a French-based online corporate travel agency. The Carlyle Group acquired a major interest in the company at its founding in 2000. In 2004, it sold the company off to IAC, a company that specialized in online travel services (expedia.com, hotels.com, etc.).[6] In an even faster turnaround, equity firm Bain Capital Management in 2005 bought Advertising Directory Solutions, a Canadian yellow pages company for $1.5 billion. It sold it to Yellow Pages Group (another Canadian company) in 2005 for $2.5 billion.

These are far-shorter turnarounds than usual, but using a longer time frame, similar scenarios are repeated over and over.

So while equity firms do seem to be turning into the conglomerates of old,[7] their real purpose is to get in, fix up, or split up, and then sell off, either to an established oligopoly in that industry or as an initial public offering (IPO) on the stock market. When it sells to a company (often a new oligopoly) that is already in the business, the equity firm acts like a catalyst in the process of oligopolization, a buffer that absorbs the lag between the time when companies are ready to sell and when others are ready to buy.

Increasingly, when a company goes on the block or splits off a division, the bidders include both direct competitors (oligopolies in the same business) and private equity companies. For example, in 2004, German technology giant Siemens AG bought out U.S. Filter, a U.S. maker of water filters, spun off by French Veolia (formerly a part of the abovementioned Vivendi, but that's another story). The $993 million deal was not a slam dunk, however. Siemens had serious competition, not from other tech firms, but from equity firms, including some of the biggest (Blackstone Group, Carlyle Group, KKR, and Warburg Pincus LLC).

Like real estate speculators, equity firms are gambling that the firms they take over will appreciate in value while they own them. Their eagerness and their almost endless supply of capital means that oligopolies are finding they have to bid ever more higher to grab the pieces that will allow them to expand their market share in a particular business. If the oligopolies trying to grow market share in their own field are not ready to buy today, they may have to spend even more to do it tomorrow.

MEASURES OF CONCENTRATION

How concentrated does an industry need to be to become an oligopoly? Two measures are commonly used by economists and antitrust regulators to judge the relative amount of concentration in any industry. They are the Concentration Ratio and the Herfindahl Hirschman Index.

Concentration Ratio

The Concentration Ratio is expressed in the format CR_x, which stands for the percentage of the market sector controlled by the biggest x firms. For example, $CR_3 = 70$ would indicate that the top-three firms control 70 percent of a market.

CR_4 is the most typical Concentration Ratio for judging what kind of an oligopoly it is. A CR_4 of over 50 is generally considered a *tight oligopoly*; CR_4 between 25 and 50 is generally considered a *loose oligopoly*. A CR_4 of under 25 is no oligopoly at all. We would add that a CR_3 of over 90 or a CR_2 of over 80 should be considered a supertight oligopoly.

The problem with this measure is that CR_4 does not indicate the relative size of the four largest companies. It may be that a CR_4 of 80 means that one company controls 50 percent of the market, while other market players have 10 percent each. That's a very different market structure than one where every firm has a 20 percent share.

Herfindahl Hirschman Index

The HHI (commonly called the Herfindahl Index) is a far more precise tool for measuring concentration. It is obtained by squaring the market share of each of the players and then adding up those squares.

The formula for this index is $[H = (\%S1)^2 + (\%S2)^2 + (\%S3)^2 + \ldots (\%Sn)^2]$. Here, %S stands for the percentages of the market owned by each of the larger companies, so that %S1 is the percentage owned by the largest company, %S2 by the second, and so on; n stands for the total number of firms you are counting.

The HHI gives added weight to the biggest companies. The higher the index, the more concentration and (within limits) the less open market competition. A pure monopoly, for example, would have an HHI index of $S1^2$ or 100^2, or 10,000. By definition, that's the maximum score. By contrast, an industry with 100 competitors, each of which has 1 percent of the market would have a score of $1^2 + 1^2 + 1^2 + \ldots 1^2$ or a total of 100.

Now that we've seen the limits, let's look at a typical situation in what economists call a *duopoly*, that is, a two-company oligopoly. If each of the two firms has a market share of 50 percent, the HHI index would be $[(50)^2 + 50^2 = 2,500 + 2,500 = 5,000]$. With two firms that have shares of 75 percent and 25 percent, respectively, the HHI index would be $[(75)^2 + (25)^2 = 5,625 + 625 = 6,250]$. In other words, the presence of a 75 percent market share for one company lifts the HHI index figure considerably. That indicates it is a more concentrated—and presumably less competitive—market.

The U.S. Antitrust Department has traditionally judged the "seriousness" of a merger by using the Herfindahl Index. According to the 1992 Merger Guidelines, a 1,000 to 1,800 HHI value generally indicates moderate concentration. Anything over 1,800 is taken to betoken acute concentration. If a merger or acquisition increases the index by 100 or more or pushes the overall index over 1,000, it is likelier to attract scrutiny from the Department of Justice.

The U.S. Census Bureau compiles a set of concentration indexes for a wide variety of industries. Unfortunately, the last version was published in 1997.[8] The next version is due out in 2006. In fact, although these make for good rough guidelines, the way in which industries are divided is, almost necessarily, too arbitrary to be definitive.

It's still quite instructive to look at these figures, although they catch only the first few years of the current decade of rapid oligopolization. For example in 1997, the top-four petroleum refining companies (CR_4) had over 41 percent market share, and the top eight companies in that area had over 57 percent. The HHI for that industry segment was 626. Tire manufacturing had figures of CR_4 = 89 percent, CR_8 = 87 percent, and an HHI of 1,667. Breakfast cereal manufacturing had a CR_3 of 82, a CR_4 of 89, and a HHI of 2,445.

Regulators look closely, as we have said, at the Herfindahl Index as a basis for deciding whether a given merger of acquisition is anticompetitive or not. In a recent case, the U.S. company Cytec Industries, which is a specialist in coatings and adhesives, announced it would buy (for $1.8 billion) the Surface Specialties unit of U.K. based UCB. The acquisitions sent up a red flag, and the Federal Trade Commission (FTC) eventually refused to accept the deal as it stood. In one specialized category, amino resins (used especially for weatherproof coatings), the two companies had a 90 percent share in the U.S. market between them. According to the FTC report, "As measured by sales, the proposed acquisition would increase concentration significantly for amino resins for industrial liquid coating and adhesion promotion in rubber, as measured by the Herfindahl Hirschman Index ('HHI'), by almost 4,000 points, to over 8,000."[9] Cytec agreed to divest the ITS amino resin holdings as a condition of the deal.

MARKET DEFINITION

This example illustrates the issue of market definition, a perennial issue with oligopolies, antitrust, and the measures of concentration. The Cytec acquisition did not bring up antitrust concerns, in general, because in the overall area of adhesives and coatings there are plenty of competitors by FTC measures. Nor was it a problem in other subcategories, such as acrylic resins. It was in the specific area of amino resins that a virtual monopoly was being created. The usual argument of the acquiring companies is that the frame of reference being challenged is too narrow.

The power to define markets is especially critical in the case of antitrust, for which the definition of market segments often makes the difference in a decision whether to oppose a merger or to ignore it. The definition of markets is by far the most important step in any antitrust lawsuit.[10]

That power can be misapplied, according to a recent article in *Forbes* magazine.[11] The author rails against the "circular logic of identifying thin markets that are—surprise!—highly concentrated." The examples cited are as follows:

- The high functioning enterprise software market—invoked in the Oracle-PeopleSoft case.
- The refrigerated pickle market—used to deny the merger of Claussen and Vlasic in 2002.
- The retail superpremium ice cream market—which affected the Nestlé-Dreyers merger in 2003, requiring that Nestlé sell off some Dreyer assets.
- The personal identification number (PIN) debit card network market—which caused First Data and Concord to sell some assets before merging in 2003.
- The spiral-bound composite can market (as used for frozen orange juice)—which stopped the merger of industry leaders Sonoco and Pasco in 2003.

Of course, at the other extreme, are broad definitions of market that would allow just about any merger to take place. Any measure of concentration only reflects the definitions with which you begin. The merger of two big phone companies such as Sprint and Nextel may have a major effect on the Concentration Ratio in the cell phone business, but it is not as significant in the larger phone industry, and a tiny one on the overall "communications" market. Even more flagrantly, the sequential mergers of phone companies SBC, AT&T, Bell South, and Cingular all passed muster from government antitrust regulators even though they created the dominant company in local phone service, long distance, business phones services, and cell phones. The existence of competition outside the traditional phone companies—namely from the cable television companies with offerings of Internet-based telephones—was considered, rather than a narrower definition of whatever industry the new AT&T entered.

BEING #1 OR #2

But it's not just the antitrust officials that define narrow segments. Companies constantly redefine market segments in which they compete so that they can tell investors and customers that they are #1 or #2 in a market. In the U.S. copier market, for example, Canon, Ricoh, and Xerox all claim to be #1, and they all define that #1 status in different ways. And all companies describe themselves as the "leader" in something or other.

However you slice the segments, companies become oligopolies because management sees a number of advantages in being industry leaders. The current orthodoxy is that being #1 or #2 in your selected markets is crucial to success.

Although he didn't originate that orthodoxy, it certainly was given its greatest currency from the ideas of former General Electric CEO Jack Welch. Of all current American industry leaders, GE most resembles a conglomerate, with interests in broadcasting, appliances, jet engines, credit, and so on. The way in which Welch kept this ungainly company with so many disparate divisions in line was through the doctrine that they would be #1 or #2 in every field they were in, or they would "fix it, sell it, or close it."[12]

Welch saw that the #1 and #2 companies can usually ride out any storm. He taught that "it was precisely the #3, #4, #5, or #6 business that suffered the most during a cyclical downturn. #1 or #2 businesses would not lose market share."[13] Or, as he is elsewhere quoted, "be #1 or #2 in your market, [because] when you're #4 or #5 in a market, you get pneumonia when #1 sneezes."[14]

This doctrine of avoiding being #3 or below has become an MBA staple, and is a commonplace practice of business journalism. Consider this quote from one now-defunct online industry news magazine: "The sharpest companies always aim to be #1 or #2 in their chosen markets—but who chooses to be #3? Or #4 or #5 or even lower down the pecking order?"

In the past few years, being #1 or #2 in a field has been the announced strategy of almost every company in every industry. Being #1 or #2 has become the hoariest cliché in company mission statements. Here are a few examples found online:

- Banking: "Banc One was strengthening its already considerable Louisiana presence by purchasing a market-share dominant player in FCC. This fit Banc One's strategic goal of being #1 or #2 in market share in geographic areas where it does business." (*Mississippi Business Journal*)
- Semiconductors: "Cypress [Semiconductor] strives to be #1 or #2 in every market, and for us to be #1 or #2 in the PLD business means we would have to displace Xilinx or Altera, and I don't think we have a path to do that,' Richardson said." (*EE Times*)
- Staffing: "The combination [with Olsten] clearly would move Adecco a long way towards its strategic objectives of being #1 or #2 in each of the major marketplaces and of reaching a 20 percent share of the industry worldwide." (Adecco press release)
- Construction equipment: "Terex (TEX) has been rapidly growing revenues and earnings both internally and through a series of focused acquisitions. The company derives half its revenues from products where it has the #1 or #2 market position." (company prospectus)
- Networking and telecom: "We're playing ... to be the #1 or #2 position in each [a 3com executive]." "We're either #1 or #2 in each one of the spaces where we play these days [a Lucent executive]." "We are #1 and #2 in almost every product area we've ever entered [a Cisco executive]." (all quoted in *Network Computing*)

- Software testing: "Our Vision [Key Labs]: Inside three years we will be #1 or #2 in every market we choose to serve." (company Web site)
- Computer gaming: "This company [Spectrum Holobyte, now owned by Infogrames SA] will continue to look for the right opportunities. We look for companies that would give us strength. We want to be a #1 or #2 player in every major entertainment category, for any major platform. If we're looking at a company to acquire, we ask ourselves the question, Would this move us to the #1 or #2 slot in a category we're already in? Will it give us the #1 or #2 slot in a category we're not in?" (interview in *Wired*)

This is a just a sampling of such declarations. The compulsion to become #1 or #2 pushes companies to get bigger at almost any price within a market segment to become one of the leaders. It also causes companies to regularly sell off divisions for which they can't conceivably become the leader and concentrate on those divisions in markets in which it can dominate.

Seen in that light, companies find themselves pulled into becoming oligopolies just to survive. It's what the managers believe, it's what the stockholders want, and in the end, it's a matter of survival.

TO SUM UP

The new oligopoly is a phenomenon of the last fifteen years. It is a strategy, only partly articulated, that businesses are following in almost every area. The new oligopoly is not a monopoly, not a conglomerate, and not usually part of a cartel.

Most, if not all, sectors of the economy are in the process of being "rolled up," as the pace of mergers and acquisitions rises. Fewer than five companies dominate everything from yogurt to farm equipment to eyeglasses. Even sectors that are traditionally disorganizing are subject to increasing concentration.

A new oligopoly strives to be #1 or #2 in its sector, and then it starts to use a position of its market domination to maintain and further its domination, as we will discuss in later chapters. To ensure a #1 or #2 position, oligopolies define the segment(s) they will dominate, usually related ones, and focus on building their dominance, through mergers and acquisitions as well as organic growth.

But oligopolies are not isolated organizations. Their existence is complicated by their concentration at other levels of their own sector and in sectors that they serve and that serve them. That is the subject of our next chapter.

2 / Oligopolies and Oligopsonies

AN *OLIGOPSONY* (UGLY WORD!) is the mirror image of an oligopoly. It is a market in which there are few *buyers*, in contrast to an oligopoly, a market where there are few *sellers*. In an oligopsony, suppliers who grow, manufacture, or create products are at the mercy of a small number of companies to which they can sell their wares or services. The oligopsonies have an easier time setting costs (what they pay for what they buy) and conditions (how the work is done) as they have few competitors bidding up the market.

MONOPSONY

Note that there is also a term *monopsony*, which is the mirror image of a monopoly—that is, a market with only one buyer. It describes a situation that is rare in the current world economy, for the same reasons that monopoly is rare (as we have discussed in the previous chapter). A monopsony, like a monopoly, would attract immediate antitrust action.

Examples of monopsonies are few. One limited monopsony is the U.S. federal government, which orders certain defense and security systems often with the condition that it be the sole client to be delivered the product, thus a monopsony. But even this is rare in the strictest sense, because security and defense advances are often sold to allied governments, and the technologies discovered are often repackaged and later sold in the private sector in a somewhat milder version.

Indeed, any government is a natural monopsony, at least in some areas. Absolutist, state-run economies, like Stalin's Soviet Union or North Korea, are dominated by monopolies and monopsonies, which often are granted to cronies by those in power. In such an economy, the cobbler or the wheat grower can, in theory, sell their products only to the government or its designated agents. In today's open commercial markets, there are next to no true large monopsonies.

Table 2.1 Key Terms

	Monopoly	Oligopoly	Oligopsony	Monopsony
Definition	One seller, many buyers	Few sellers, many buyers	Many sellers, few buyers	Many sellers, one buyer
Occurrence	Rare	Frequent	Frequent	Rare
Examples	Some local utilities, Microsoft (almost)	Movie studios, airplane manufacturers, iron-ore miners	U.S. beef processors, banana shippers, airplane manufacturers	National governments (locally), absolutist economies
Leverage over	Prices	Prices (within limits)	Costs (within limits), standards	Costs, standards

There can be local monopsonies as well, such as when a single company dominates transport, the way that individual U.S. railroads once did to locations inhabited by American farmers. The railroads notoriously could charge "all the traffic will bear,"[1] meaning whatever they could squeeze out of the farmers who had no other way of getting their wheat or cattle to market. A similar principle applies to airline tickets when a small city is served by only one airline.

To sum up these key terms, see Table 2.1.

EXAMPLES OF OLIGOPSONY

Oligopsony, although rarely discussed, is a common situation in the real economy. Here are a few examples of a situation in which there are few buyers:

- If you grow cocoa beans in the Ivory Coast or Indonesia, for example, there are a small number of worldwide companies (Archer Daniels Midland, Cargill, and Callebaut) that might buy your product. These companies essentially dictate prices, market timing, and specifications (what size, quality, and subspecies of cocoa beans they will accept).
- If you are a U.S. cattle rancher, there are really only five major meat-packing companies that you can sell your beef to (Tyson Foods, Cargill, Swift, U.S. Premium Beef, and Smithfield Foods). Yes, there are a few independents, such as small local or specialty meatpackers, but the vast majority of all meat sold is sold through these big five, and you'll have to bargain with them if you run a cattle-growing operation.
- If you sell any kind of airplane equipment or supplies, your sales force will be desperate to get orders from Boeing, EADS, Lockheed Martin, and a handful of other companies worldwide.

OLIGOPSONY

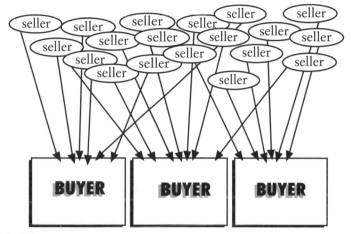

Figure 2.1 Oligopsony.
Artist: Andrew Hoffman

- If you are a heart surgeon or a gynecologist, you are increasingly sell-ing your services, not to a large number of patients, but to a small and decreasing number of health insurance companies and managed care plans (such as Aetna, UnitedHealth, and Anthem). Those insurance companies have the power of setting rates and conditions, questioning your medical decisions, and restricting your choices, especially as fewer and fewer companies dominate in any one region.
- The companies that develop software for mobile phones in the United States basically must sell to four companies: Verizon, Cingular, Sprint Nextel, and T-Mobile. Lose a contract to one of these companies (as Infospace, which supplies entertainment and directories to cell phone users, did in 2006 with Cingular), and you risk losing your company.

EMPLOYMENT OLIGOPSONIES

Employees "sell" their work to employers; employers "buy" that work. The amount of real competition between employers for certain employees is a criti-cal factor in determining pay and benefits. Some employment oligopsonies are local ones. Towns in which only one industry has decent pay enable that employer to create a local oligopsony. But that condition (the so-called com-pany town), common in earlier centuries and in less developed countries, is less common in industrial companies where workers have greater mobility. And as China is now experiencing,[2] a mobile workforce drives wages upward.

But employees in many trades or professions are limited by the number of buyers of their services. Nursing is a good example of this trend.[3] In most areas in the United States, most top nursing jobs are controlled by a limited set of hospitals. The larger the number of employable nurses and the smaller the number of hospitals competing for their services, the lower the compensation. Oligopsonists are given the opportunity to exploit labor conditions by keeping wages and benefits at lower levels (a buyer's market). If, as is currently the case, there is a general shortage of nurses, compensations eventually rise (a seller's market).

Organized labor is, among other things, an attempt to limit the power of oligopsonies to dictate wages, benefits, and conditions. U.S. public schoolteachers, for example, especially in states where they can resist being replaced by strikebreakers, have a decisive input in setting wages and working conditions, something that unorganized nurses (generally) do not have.

Athletes are a vivid example of the role unions can have in breaking employment oligopsonies. In baseball,[4] for example, the oligopsony of major league teams was historically used to keep salaries low, even those of star players. Players were like indentured servants with no option to choose their employers, and the owners were in agreement to uphold that rule. In 1976 the baseball players union won a court decision allowing them to engage in collective bargaining. The result was that players were allowed to become free agents, and teams had to actively compete for the services of veteran players. Over the next ten years, average player salaries went up over 500 percent[5] and have gone higher since.

But even unions do not offer absolute protections. The recent lowering of wages and salaries for all unionized employees of traditional U.S. airlines (Delta, United, and others) has been accomplished under the threat of imminent bankruptcy and the understanding that no comparable jobs are available at the discount airlines. For example, in 2006, Northwest Airlines got a giveback of 24 percent on average from its pilots, and that came after a 2004 salary cutback of 14 percent.[6]

Likewise, Ford and General Motors have been able to get (minimal) concessions from once all-powerful unions as they threaten bankruptcy. These include larger employee contributions to health care costs and retiree benefits. With U.S. automakers in big financial trouble, much bigger givebacks (or a massive strike) are in the works. If the unions are cooperating even a little, it's because no comparable jobs are available for their workers. As oligopsony buyers of highly paid union laborers, the auto companies and airlines are using the threat of bankruptcy (and the loss of all higher-paying jobs) to get concessions.

MIDDLEMEN

Oligopsonies often act as middlemen. In many other cases, although you as a producer eventually are selling to large numbers of consumers, your chances of reaching large numbers are decided by a small number of firms that act as middlemen. Let's say you and your garage rock band cuts a CD. While there may be millions of potential listeners for your product out in the world, you can only reach them in a big way through a limited number of music companies. These are the few companies that can get your songs airplay, arrange publicity, and set tour dates. After all, other acts are just as eager to get distributed on the label, so they can pick and choose. In any negotiations, they have the upper hand. (And, yes, a few bands do pretty well even without a big label, by building recognition on the Web, but these are exceptions.)

At one time, many of these middlemen bought your product directly and resold it to others. Now, increasingly, they are more likely to work a deal by which they receive the products on consignment and take only indirect responsibility for selling them.

All grocery stores work this way. If you want national sales, you bring your new salsa product to Kroger, Safeway, 7-Eleven, and Wal-Mart. In general, however, you either have to pay them so-called stocking fees to even consider putting your product on the shelves or agree to other strict conditions (delivery times, margins, promotions) to get room in the store. You can continue to sell the product through small local retailers or via mail order, but if you want wider distribution, you'll run up against the demands of those who own the biggest chains.

If you sell drywall, power tools, or sink fixtures, your salesmen will be trying to get time with the buyers at Home Depot, Lowe's, and other home improvement chains. Yes, you can sell to smaller hardware chains or lumber yards, but those outlets are getting fewer in number as local hardware companies are wiped out by the big-box stores. If you deal with the oligopsony, you'll lose your ability to dictate price and determine specifications.

So, too, with the book industry. Barnes & Noble and Borders (along with Wal-Mart again) sell a majority of books in the United States. If you are a publisher, you have to deal with them. That gives them a lot of power over how and when they pay you and who swallows incidental costs.[7] In fact, those chains are notorious for taking their time paying publishers and for immediately giving the heave-ho to anything that is not selling fast enough. They could make even further demands on the publishers, as noted in a *Village Voice* article: "Backed by financial muscle and heavy inventories, chains demanded lower wholesale prices to deeply discount bestsellers—a practice that had previously been illegal until the final repeal of anti-monopoly fair trade laws in 1975. Chains also wanted more co-op money—the product placement fees publishers pay for prominent display."[8]

OLIGOPSONIES AS GATEKEEPERS

Book publishing is an example of a specific form of oligopsony. The media companies determine which books, music, and video receive wide public exposure. These companies pay for usage rights and are the gatekeepers to the public.

- There are now basically four recording companies in the world (Universal Music Group, Sony BMG, EMI, and Warner Music Group). As noted above, if you're a musician or a producer and you want to be heard widely, you have to deal with the big four, which previously were the big six, then the big five, and are now threatening to become the big three as pressures to consolidate increase and as a policy of more permissive antitrust regulation emerges. These companies essentially decide what music gets recorded, what gets marketed, and what is budgeted. To a certain extent, they dictate what the public gets to choose between. It's true that they are losing market power, thanks to digital piracy and consumer dissatisfaction with their offerings, but they are still the gatekeepers to the music world.

- Clear Channel and CBS own a major portion of all radio stations in the United States and dominate most of the top markets. If you are a recording company wanting to "sell" a song for airtime, you have to deal with them (and that has sometimes meant *payola*, a kind of stocking fee). These radio companies, although their power is fading (thanks to satellite radio, iPods, and their own tired formats), are the gatekeepers that stand between you and your audience.

- Six companies own almost all of the networks and cable stations on U.S. TV sets—Disney, News Corporation (Fox), General Electric (NBC), Viacom, CBS (newly separated from Viacom), and Time Warner. If you want to sell programming, there are few alternatives. These companies determine what programs will run, so if you want to produce a TV show, you almost have to talk to people from these companies. They pretty well determine what viewers get to choose.

- If you have a brilliant idea for a movie, you'll probably want to talk to someone in one of the big six movie studios—Sony, Fox, Disney, Universal (NBC), Paramount (Viacom), and Warner Bros. Entertainment. But you have an idea that doesn't require Brad Pitt, a cast of thousands, or exploding spaceships, so you'll want to talk to the independent studios. But wait a minute! Most of them are owned by the same big studios.

- So you produce your film yourself. Then you see that four companies own the majority of the movie theater screens in the United States— AMC Theaters, Regal Entertainment Group, Cinemark, and Carmike Cinemas. If you want to distribute a film, you have to deal with these four companies. In a sense, they are your first "buyer" for the film; they, in turn, sell seats to the general public. No problem if you are a big studio that will promote the film with a multimillion dollar marketing budget and bankable stars. If you are a small distributor with a minimal budget, however, you'll have great trouble accessing more than a few independent art house screens. Independent producers have tried to get around this by going direct to TV or to DVD. But what station is interested in showing a film no one has seen? And what store is going to stock a DVD that has not the slightest buzz? (We'll talk more about the movie oligopoly in Chapter 8.)

Oligonomies and the Long Tail

Chris Anderson's 2006 book *The Long Tail*[9] has received a lot of well-deserved attention. He explains how the Internet has changed the market for all kinds of goods simply by bringing down the cost of inventory and marketing and making it possible to sell effectively to niche group members who are actively looking for products that have no mass-market appeal. It celebrates the triumph of the back list, where movies, CDs, and books that were at one time uneconomical to store and sell because of their low individual sales volume have now become a viable business. It is now possible to reach a worldwide audience of potential buyers with focused interests. Those audiences, cumulatively, are enormous, and companies have proven that you can make a living selling highly niched products.

What this means is that the obstacles in the way of getting shelf space are, to an extent, being eliminated. You can bypass the supermarket buyer, the music company, the book publisher, and the TV networks, and open your own direct channels. From a consumer point of view, you are no longer limited by the books currently in stock at your local Borders, the songs played on Clear Channel stations, or the DVDs stocked by Blockbuster.

But I believe Anderson goes astray on some points. It's ironic that the book proclaiming the end of the "hit-based" economy was released in the same month as the hit movie *Pirates of the Caribbean: Dead Man's Chest* opened. That film was one of the biggest hits of all time, bringing in $422 million in its theatrical release, as well as the having highest first-day opening ever. Nobody told Disney executives that the age of "hit-driven economics" is over. Nor were Anderson's publishers, Hyperion (also a division of Disney) unhappy to see the book making the best-seller lists (unlike most books that have only a few readers).

More important, the book presents a vision of a crowded market with lots of competition from small companies. In some ways it is true that books, CDs, and even exotic teas from smaller companies all have a chance to generate some business. The people who want their products will find them. At the same time, however, the "Long Tail" has generated its own powerful oligopolies,

Companies often cited in the book—including NetFlix, iTunes, Rhapsody, Amazon, eBay, and even Google—are new oligopolies (and in cases like eBay and Google almost monopolies) that are replacing looser retail oligopolies in some areas. True, these companies are kinder to some small businesses, the small publishers, moviemakers, and record labels; however, they are also further speeding the demise of the local bookstore, record store, or movie rental outlet.

Critic John Cassidy, in his *New Yorker* review of the book, noted this return of market domination in the guise of the new economy:

> Today, thanks to globalization, deregulation, and technological progress, many of the twentieth-century industrial behemoths have fallen by the wayside. But don't assume that giant, exploitative firms are a thing of the past. In recent years, eBay has sharply increased its commission rates; Amazon has admitted charging its customers different prices for the same goods; and Apple Computer has stubbornly refused to make its iTunes service compatible with portable music players other than iPods. Has the New Economy really moved past the familiar "winner take all" dynamic? That depends on whether you're looking at the long tail—or at who's wagging it."[10]

Some people believe that the Internet has changed everything, but except in the troubled music industry, the gatekeepers are alive and well, "long tail" or not.

SQUEEZING SUPPLIERS

The big advantage of being part of an oligopsony is a unique opportunity to squeeze your suppliers. In some ways, that's even more advantageous than oligopolies' ability to set prices, because it all happens out of the public eye.

A *Wall Street Journal* article called "Bully Buyers"[11] explains how oligopsonies are becoming a major antitrust issue.[12] As the article states, oligopsony as a legal issue is nothing new, "but it is getting more attention now because of the rise of giant companies in a global marketplace. Buyer muscle has become more visible in recent years as markets become more concentrated through mergers and joint ventures."

Among the examples cited in the article that have led to legal action are the following:

- Four big processors conspired to keep down what they would pay for Maine blueberries.
- Several paper companies conspired to "depress softwood prices" in South Carolina, lowering them by 35 percent.
- Insurance companies in Alabama and Pennsylvania imposed contracts that forced down doctor and hospital fees.
- In the tobacco industry, cigarette companies (we bow down to two big ones in the United States—Philip Morris and Reynolds American) apparently conspired to lower what they would pay tobacco farmers by agreeing not to bid against each other at tobacco auctions. The article quotes one well-known auctioneer as stating that "despite the appearance of active bidding there's been virtually no price competition since the mid-1990s."[13] (The tobacco companies settled out of court for $200 million in 2003.)

WAL-MART SQUEEZES HARDEST

Wal-Mart, unsurprisingly, comes up in that same *Wall Street Journal* article, which contests the current antitrust thinking that, because Wal-Mart reduces prices to the consumer, anything it does must by definition be healthy for the economy. The idea that price-cutting is always good means that the government is oblivious to most activities on the cost side.

Wal-Mart, of course, is a notorious squeezer of its suppliers, demanding constantly lower prices and ever more services to Wal-Mart. As one critic puts it, "The Wal-Mart squeeze means vendors have to be as relentless and as microscopic as Wal-Mart is at managing their own costs. They need, in fact, to turn themselves into shadow versions of Wal-Mart itself."[14] Some argue that

Wal-Mart's unrelenting pressure is actually good for the economy and that the company has been almost single-handedly responsible for U.S. productivity gains over the past few decades,[15] simply by forcing its suppliers to become more efficient. On the other hand, the Wal-Mart squeeze, which usually starts as a warm embrace, has been the doom or near-doom of companies who have been squeezed until they could give no more.

And, of course, this squeezing is passed along—to employees[16] whose wages get lowered or whose jobs are sent offshore, to suppliers of the suppliers who get beaten up in turn, and to customers who get lower-quality products.

The suppliers are in a tough place, according to Charles Fishman, author of *The Wal-Mart Effect*, a sober assessment of Wal-Mart and its effect on the economy. He writes, "Companies doing 10 percent or less of their business with Wal-Mart had operating profit margins of 12.7 percent. Companies that become 'captive suppliers' to Wal-Mart—selling more than 25 percent of their goods to Wal-Mart—see their profit margin cut almost in half, to 7.3 percent."[17]

COUNTERVAILING POWER

You can't negotiate very well if the company you are talking with is enormous and you are tiny. But if you are Shaw Industries, the #1 maker of carpets in the world, if you want to negotiate with Home Depot or Lowe's, you'll certainly get your calls answered and you'll have something to bargain with. Similarly, Procter & Gamble or Coca-Cola can, to some extent, stand up against Wal-Mart, Target, or Walgreens, which need to offer some of their key products or they'll risk losing customers. Smaller companies don't have a chance. It's hard enough for many of them to get a contract with a big company, let alone have a meaningful dialogue about terms and conditions.

That's why in the end many excellent small companies with innovative products have trouble surviving as independent companies. No matter how good their products (unless they are unique), they'll have to swallow the conditions of one of these middlemen unless they can somehow appeal directly to potential buyers. It's a lot easier to sell your operation to a company that already has clout.

SOY MILK HITS THE SHELVES

A good example of this phenomenon is soy milk. Soy milk has been a fixture at health food stores and has existed for many years, but you'd have been lucky to find it in the grocery stores in the 1990s. In 2002, the leading soy milk company (WhiteWave Foods) was bought out by the leading dairy company in the world, U.S.-based Dean Foods (which owns such brands as Borden, Land O'Lakes, and more than a score of leading local dairies under various names). Dean had the market muscle to get soy milk, under the brand name Silk, prominently displayed in almost all supermarkets and grocery stores and in every Starbucks. Silk comes in a half-dozen flavors and variations, which now have their own row in most supermarket refrigerator cases alongside the skim and 2 percent milk.

The point is that Dean Foods already had massive power as a $10 billion a year company, and Dean Foods' executives could get Safeway (a $38 billion company) and Starbucks (a $6 billion company) executives to return their phone calls, and it was easy to add the Silk products to the array of products they were already delivering. By comparison, even a very successful $100 or $200 million a year company like WhiteWave Foods, no matter how inventive, is way down the priority list for multibillion dollar supermarket chains. As part of a countervailing oligopoly, Dean Foods can sit across the table from an oligopoly and have a meaningful bargaining session.

OLIGOPSONIES GENERATE OLIGOPOLIES AND VICE VERSA

Contrarily, oligopsonies are formed to fight the power of the oligopolies. In industry after industry, concentration at one level leads to concentration at another, as companies through merger, acquisition, and restructuring are themselves getting bigger to counteract the power of oligopolies or oligopsonies they have to deal with.

For example, the world iron-ore mining industry is dominated by three multinational companies; whereas up until recently, the steel industry, comprising its principal customers, was divided into dozens of small and midsize national companies. The iron-ore companies—Rio Tinto (an Anglo-Australian company), CVRD (Brazil), and BHP Billiton (Australia)—have had their way in the last few years in negotiating ever higher prices, threatening to leave any companies that refuse to pay the new going rate without a source of ore.[18] One reaction in the steel industry has been an increasing wave of mergers both national (as the number of Chinese steel companies keeps decreasing through mergers) and international (where #1 Mittal Steel recently bought #2 Arcelor). A reaction to iron-ore oligopoly is not the only reason for the concentration in the steel market, but it certainly has to be a significant one.

Hospitals, too, continue to get bigger so they can stand up against insurance companies. It was the demands of concentrating health insurance companies in the Boston area that forced hospitals to combine operations. According to a *Wall Street Journal* story,[19] Boston hospitals, once fiercely independent, steadily concentrated, from 34 to 12 hospital networks over the course of a decade. The reason: the ability to fight back against ever-fewer and more demanding health insurers. And when one big regional insurer (Tufts Health Plan) balked at the prices of the elite world-famous hospitals in the area (Massachusetts General and Brigham and Women's Hospital) and threatened to stop paying for patients who elected to use them, local customers and the affected, now united, hospitals were able to bring enough power and prestige to compel a compromise. The recently merged hospital group had much more leverage with the insurers than it would have had as isolated institutions and worked out a solution that both sides could live with.

Cooperatives Fight Back

A well-honed approach to fighting oligopsonies with oligopolies is the establishment of sellers' cooperatives, seen mostly in agriculture and fishing. The cooperatives are an alliance between small farmers or fishermen who see collective action as the best way to avoid getting crushed by oligopsonistic buyers.

Agricultural cooperatives were enabled by the 1922 Capper-Volstead Act, which allowed farmers an exemption from antitrust regulation when they come into voluntary association for processing and marketing their goods. Such cooperatives tend to work best when they can stand firm against a food-selling oligopoly.

One of the most successful cooperatives has been Ocean Spray, made up of 800 cranberry and grapefruit farmers. In 2006, the group signed a single-source supply contract with PepsiCo (who markets Ocean Spray–brand beverages), but because of their cooperative status they came up with a far-better deal than they could ever have gotten as individual growers.[20]

Dairy cooperatives, apple-growing cooperatives, maple syrup cooperatives, as well as corn, soybean, and wheat cooperatives all allow farmers to combine their bargaining power when dealing with the biggest buyers.

But cooperatives have no magic protection against mismanagement. Farmland Industries was the cooperative of all cooperatives. Founded in 1929, it was owned by 1,700 regional cooperatives, representing 600,000 member farmers. Primarily in the pork and beef business and a Fortune 500 company, it declared bankruptcy in 2002 in a spectacular flame-out based on mismanagement, termed in a pending lawsuit[21] as "gross negligence and acts of corporate waste." Its meatpacking assets were sold off to two oligopolies—Smithfield Foods (pork) and U.S. Premium Beef—and it continues as a much-diminished group.

The growth of cooperatives can have its own anticompetitive aspects. "Some cooperatives have consolidated or in other ways grown to a size providing countervailing power against large private firms. In fact, the size and predatory conduct of some large cooperatives has drawn the attention of antitrust agencies in recent decades."[22]

For example, in 2004, the U.S. Justice Department settled an action against the Eastern Mushroom Marketing Cooperative, the nation's largest mushroom farmer cooperative, which has been buying up rival farms and closing them down, something called "supply control," an antitrust no-no.

Oligopsony buyers can undermine agricultural cooperatives through imports. The biggest U.S. soybean processors (Cargill, Archer Daniels Midland, and Bunge) are now importing soybeans and processed soy products from the burgeoning Brazilian market, putting ever more pressure on U.S. growers and their cooperatives. The same is becoming true of beef and corn, raised and grown in central Brazil, which only a few decades ago was considered to be a wasteland. In similar ways, local growers cooperatives in countries like Guatemala are being squeezed off the shelves of the burgeoning local supermarkets owned by multinational oligopolies like Ahold and Wal-Mart. Those companies bring in cheaper and more standardized foods from Mexico, Brazil, or even the United States.

In other industries, similar examples abound. Fewer supermarkets mean fewer food brokers and wholesalers to serve them. The concentration in state-wide textbook approval boards has led to a concentration in textbook publishers. In the agricultural sector, the decreasing number of buyers to sellers has resulted in a renewed interest in cooperatives.

MARKET TIERS AND "OLIGONOMIES"

In the real world, oligopolies and oligopsonies rarely exist in isolation. As a market develops, a set of interlocking oligopolies and oligopsonies arises. This organization means the evolution of a company that is an oligopoly in one direction and an oligopsony in the other.

The vocabulary of economists has no word to describe that increasingly common phenomenon. An increasing number of market sectors include companies that are both an oligopoly and an oligopsony. We call this an *oligonomy.*[23]

In an oligonomy, companies act as an oligopoly to one group and as an oligopsony to another. The book industry, greatly simplified, works as laid out in Table 2.2.

A handful of major book publishers—owned by media companies like Viacom, Bertelsmann, News Corp, and Pearson) account for over 80 percent of book sales. They act as a kind of oligopsony to authors, who are unorganized and, except in a few cases, have little power to command prompt payment or anything else. These book publishers sell through a limited number of major booksellers (Barnes & Noble, Borders, Amazon). The book publishers are a weak oligopoly (too many books published and too many potential smaller competitors), and the booksellers are a strong oligopsony. And the big three booksellers are an oligopoly to the readers.

A More Complex Oligonomy

A much more complex oligonomy exists in the $20 billion game console business, represented by the big three console makers: Sony (PlayStation), Microsoft (Xbox) and Nintendo (GameCube and others) Between them they have essentially a 100 percent share of the market.

A simplified map of the game console oligonomy (hardware side only) is shown in Table 2.3.

Table 2.2 Five-Tiered Book Oligonomy

Authors
Agents
Book publishers
Booksellers
Readers

OLIGONOMY

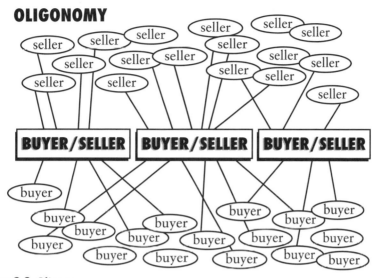

Figure 2.2 Oligonomy.
Artist: Andrew Hoffman.

The big three console makers are an oligopsony to their components suppliers. For example, Microsoft has had its consoles assembled by Taiwan's Wistron NeWeb Corporation, which in turn buys subcomponents from Walsin Technology (capacitors), Sunon (fans), Ji Haw (power cables), FoxLink (connectors), Phoenix Precision Technology (chip substrate), Taiwan Semiconductor, and ASE (semiconductors), just to name a few. Many are Taiwan-based companies, and some have Chinese manufacturing facilities. Sony and Nintendo have similar supply chains.

In this case, Microsoft is an oligopsony to its main supplier, who in turn is part of an oligopsony to its suppliers. In a small way, a company like Wistron is an oligopoly, because few companies can put together the logistics and manufacturing skill to make these consoles in time and on budget. But clearly Wistron needs Microsoft much more than Microsoft needs it.

On the other side, Microsoft is an oligopoly supplier of a valuable commodity, game boxes. It doesn't sell directly to consumers, but rather through retailers, predominantly big-box retailers like Best Buy, Circuit City, and (inevitably) Wal-Mart,

Table 2.3 Six-Tiered Game Console Oligonomy

Suppliers to subcomponent makers
Subcomponent makers
Assemblers and manufacturers
Game console companies
Big-box retailers and online retailers
Consumers

Table 2.4 Five-Tiered Beef Oligonomy

Ranchers
Feedlots
Beef packers
Supermarkets
Shoppers

along with online stores. On the other hand, the top retailers form an oligopsony, so Microsoft can't take them for granted either. So we see more of a meeting of equals when Microsoft's and Best Buys' people sit down to discuss availability and margins.

Beef Industry

The five big beef packers buy their beef, for the most part, from feedyards who complete the fattening process. To the feedlots, the beef giants constitute an oligopsony, and the feedlots are at a disadvantage to them. In turn, the feedlots, act as an oligopsony to the ranchers and farmers who raise the steers for the first five to ten months. And as the feedlot industry has concentrated, it can act as an oligopoly (although a weaker one) to the beef packers. In turn, the beef packers are oligopolies to the supermarkets that resell the meat they produce, with a bargaining advantage over those retailers. The biggest supermarkets get bigger so they can form an oligopsony to oppose the beef packers. The supermarkets in turn act as oligopolies to shoppers. This relationship is mapped in Table 2.4.

This is a simplified portrait of a five-tier oligonomy, where a few firms basically dominate each layer that comes between producers and consumers. We might add the relationship between beef packers and food service companies who supply smaller restaurant companies, and between beef packers and big chains like McDonald's and Burger King.

More Examples

When several layers of the market are defined by a series of oligopsonies and oligopolies, we have a tiered oligonomy, a sort of "Dagwood sandwich" of layer after layer. Some examples follow:

- A small number of health insurers act as oligopolies to the companies that buy their group plans for their employees. In turn, they act as oligopsonies toward the hospitals, drug companies, wheelchair makers, and other health providers whose services and products their insured members buy. This is a typical oligonomy, where the insurance companies have an advantage in both directions. But what happens next turns it into a tiered oligonomy—hospitals combine forces in hospital

Table 2.5 Grocery Oligonomy

Suppliers (farmers, etc.)
Small food manufacturers
Brokers
Supermarkets
Shoppers

groups to stand tall against the insurance companies. Likewise the drug companies and medical supplies companies get bigger so they can present strong oligopolies to insurance oligopsonies.

- Safeway, Kroger, and Wal-Mart are part of a grocery oligopoly to shoppers. To large food producers and food brokers, they are oligopsonies. In turn, food brokers act as oligopolies to the supermarkets. To the small food producers (that is, those with only a few products who can't deal directly with Safeway or Wal-Mart), they act as oligopsonies. The whole system is a tiered oligonomy. And we can extend that. The few vendors, for example, that package ice cream (Nestlé, Unilever) are an oligopsony to dairy farmers who produce cream and an oligopoly to the supermarkets who sell ice cream (see Table 2.5).
- In the global chocolate industry, basically three companies (Archer Daniels Midland, Cargill, and Callebaut) buy and process most of the cocoa beans. They are an oligopsony to the farmers in West Africa, Central America, and Brazil. In turn, they act as an oligopoly to the chocolate manufacturers. There are four major chocolate producers (Nestlé, Kraft, Mars, and Hershey's). These four act as an oligopsony to the cocoa merchants, and they act as an oligopoly to the shops and markets that sell their candy. And the big supermarkets, in turn, become an oligopsony/oligopoly (see Table 2.6).

OLIGONOMIES BREED OLIGONOMIES

The formation of tiered oligonomics helps explain the rapid concentration in most industries. A new oligopoly or oligopsony restores, to some extent, balance between layers of the market. Wal-Mart can't dictate to Coca-Cola, nor can Coca-Cola dictate to Wal-Mart. But in most cases, two distinct groups are left out of any oligonomy.

Table 2.6 Chocolate Oligonomy

Cocoa growers
Cocoa processors (Cargill, Callebaut)
Chocolate makers (Nestlé, Kraft, Mars, Hershey's)
Retailers
Chocolate eaters

Individual end users (shoppers, patients, TV watchers) have only one power in an oligonomy, that of refusing to buy (easier done when buying candy or watching TV than when having an appendix removed). But such a boycott is hard to organize and to sustain. On the other hand, the workers or small producers who are at the other end of the oligonomy have little power. The cocoa grower, the dairy farmer, the nurse, the semiconductor technician have little leverage in the oligonomy. Exceptions include (as we have noted) growers associations and trade unions; however, in the United States, trade unions have been losing ground fast in the last twenty years and agricultural cooperatives have a mixed record.

In fact, the big oligopsonies now actively undermine any attempt at organization with threats of exclusion and harassment. If banana growers in Guatemala organize to raise prices, the banana oligopsony will move to Costa Rica, Colombia, or some other banana-producing country and shut out the Guatemalans.[24] If workers organize at a Wal-Mart store, Wal-Mart will close the store and set up a new one with new employees nearby.

Just like oligopolies, oligonomies are spreading in almost every market and market segment. Being both an oligopoly and an oligopsony is an advantageous position. But it is also, for many companies, a necessary survival move.

In every market, fewer and bigger competitors at any level attain leverage in their dealings with those above and below them in the tiered oligonomy. Gaining that power is a gigantic reason why making mergers and acquisitions has become as important a part of a company's agenda as improving the products or the marketing campaign. Becoming an oligonomy is the sweet spot for big companies.

ONLY THE BIG CAN SERVE THE BIG

Although cornering the market and imperial ambitions are often motives for massive mergers and acquisitions, for companies in service industries, such deals are simply a matter of survival. As their clients become multinational and massive, so too must the companies that serve them or else face losing their business.

In the retail area, this kind of just-on-time supply response is something that no small company can do as well as a big company. Companies that sell products through large national chains need a twenty-four-hour staff and a sophisticated information technology (IT) and warehousing program to respond to every swing in the market. Imagine, for example, a sudden understock of size 13 of a particular athletic-shoe brand in a Foot Locker outlet at a shopping mall in Schaumburg, Illinois. Making sure that specific model is on the truck and at the store tomorrow is critical to profitability. It is not something a small manufacturer of sneakers can respond to. It is important to the Foot Locker chain that that shortfall, and hundreds of thousands like it every day, are handled without any extra time or overhead. Only few big suppliers (Nike, Adidas—which now owns Reebok—and New Balance) with national presence, a major logistics operation, and a fleet of trucks can afford to respond to that challenge. That's a hurdle smaller companies can't surmount.

It's a matter of efficiency. Take a company like Procter & Gamble. With operations in over 100 countries and in a score of product segments, it makes no sense for the company to have to coordinate the efforts of local services in each country and each segment. When Danone Group wants to put together a new advertising campaign worldwide for its yogurt and biscuits, it hires an ad agency (in this case, The Grey Group) with worldwide reach and expertise in national markets, rather than having to hire a separate agency for each of the over 100 countries in which it sells.

In fact, more and more large companies are looking for single suppliers, awarding one contract for a certain service nationally and often internationally. This approach has its problems, because it makes the company overly dependent on one other company. But even companies that retreat from a single-supplier solution reduce the number of companies that they deal with to a few.[25]

A company like Procter & Gamble needs to have a coordinated worldwide patent application and protection strategy, so that its Pringles products are protected in South Africa as well as its shampoo brands are in Lithuania. To manage this in detail would take an enormous internal staff. Much better to coordinate with one or two law firms that specialize in patents, who in turn will have either branch offices or associates from Caracas to Canberra. This can be achieved only by a law firm with the same global reach as its client. The law firms don't need to have offices in every capital in the world, but they must be able to coordinate the work of local experts in every country.

The big multinational corporations want to minimize the number of transactions it takes them to get something done, whether it be public relations, accounting, money management, travel booking, air freight, recruiting, printing, or environmental issues. But no company wants to keep a full staff of people who are not involved in the core business, if it can outsource the work. Hence, the proliferation of worldwide service firms.

Some examples follow:

- The growth of global banks, insurance companies, and other financial services with worldwide reach. Citigroup and HSBC are the models, with branches almost everywhere and expertise in the local business climate and regulations in every country. Increasingly, you can't even play the game with the biggest companies unless you can provide a full range of financial services in Bucharest and Bangkok as easily as you can in Boston.
- An explosion in the size and reach of major law firms.
- The dominance of the big four accounting firms (Ernst & Young, KPMG, Deloitte & Touche, and PricewaterhouseCoopers), the only ones who have the expertise and the bodies to deal with the biggest corporations.

Law Firms Get Big to Serve the Big

Consolidation in one industry, as we have noted, leads to consolidation in other industries. This trend is particularly marked in business services.

Law firms have the same issues, and the result has been an explosion in mergers over the past decade. According to consulting service Hildebrandt International,[26] law firm mergers have in the last few years proceeded at record levels. As their report notes,

> What is particularly notable about recent mergers is the increasing size and complexity of the transactions. General practice firms in major markets are increasingly feeling that 150–300 lawyers is only mid-sized, both from the perspective of clients and recruits. Consequently, many of these firms are exploring expansion opportunities.[27]

Among the reasons given for expansion are expanding geographic reach, the ability to service bigger clients, the ability to recruit better staff, and the ability to extend the firm's reach in such specialties as technology, intellectual property, or international trade. So local firms become regional, regional firms become national, and national firms go international.

One Atlanta lawyer whose firm was looking for merger partners was quoted as stating,

> There is a sense that you've got to be a certain mass, a certain size, to be attractive to the larger clientele, the bigger corporations. . . . Business is so competitive with lawyers coming to clients from so many different angles; a lot of firms conclude that they can't be stuck in the middle.[28]

International law firms were once rare, but in the past few years, there have been several major U.S.-U.K. mergers, creating large firms with transatlantic expertise. Other firms are eager to gain expertise in Chinese or Indian law, as increasing numbers of their biggest clients are more deeply involved in those countries. The mergers go both ways. Major U.S. firms have been taken over by British firms, and vice versa, and the European Union is making the merger of European law firms all the more essential.

Acquisitions act as a shortcut that avoids the need to hire experts and develop a specialist practice lawyer by lawyer. The scramble to get big fast is happening all over the legal profession. Increasingly, the most effective way to do that is to buy the desired talent by acquiring a specialist firm, rather than take years—which the increasingly competitive legal marketplace won't allow—to develop its own expertise.

All these mergers and acquisitions are changing the nature of law practice both nationally and internationally. It wasn't so long ago that a law firm with over 200 lawyers was rare. Today, firms with 500 lawyers are commonplace—over 70 such firms are based in the United States alone.

Some big firms include the following:[29]

- Clifford Chance, LLP, which is generally considered to be the world's largest law firm, has over 3,500 lawyers on staff, offices in 20 countries, and multinational oligopoly clients like Pfizer, Siemens, and Citigroup. The law firm is the result of a 2000 merger between the U.K.'s Clifford Chance, the U.S.'s Rogers & Wells, and Germany's Pünder Volhard Weber & Axster.

- Chicago-based Baker & McKenzie LLP employs over 3,200 lawyers, has clients like Microsoft and Verizon, and operates in 35 countries, with extensive operations in both Russia and China.
- New York–based Skadden, Arps, Slate, Meagher & Flom LLP employs over 1,800 lawyers with clients including Tyson Foods, DaimlerChrysler, and Warner-Lambert.
- Cleveland-based Jones, Day, Reavis & Pogue LLP has over 1,800 attorneys on its staff, and clients like General Motors, Nabisco, and BP.
- Chicago-based Sideley, Austin, Brown & Wood LLP has over 1,500 lawyers, clients like General Electric and RR Donnelley, and a major presence in Japan and China.
- Los Angeles–based Latham & Watkins has over 1,600 attorneys, staffs offices from Moscow to Tokyo, and represents such companies as Nike, Wells Fargo, Safeway, and Lehman Brothers.
- New York–based White & Case has nearly 1,600 attorneys on staff, offices in 25 countries, and such clients as Sun Microsystems, Yukos, and Deutsche Bank.

These firms aren't growing just for the fun of it. They are getting bigger because their clients have needs that can only be attended to with an ever-larger phalanx of lawyers in different locations and with different specialties.

- International commercial real estate firms for renting office space throughout the world (Cushman & Wakefield, CBRE, and Trammel Crowe).
- The rise of major technical consulting practices to provide worldwide IT consulting (IBM, HP, Cisco, Accenture, and AT&T). These matters have gotten too complex for local companies or in-house staff to manage. You must be able to put together a project team in Bangalore as fast as you can get one to Boise. That means having people who know the local customs and language and who can take the headaches away from the hiring company.
- The growth of worldwide advertising and public relations groups, using a variety of more specialized semi-independent subgroups (Omnicom, WPP, Interpublic, and Publicis).
- The growth of staffing and temporary work companies internationally (Addecco, Manpower, and Randstad Employment).
- The globalization of delivery services and freight companies. FedEx, UPS, and DHL have gone global and they offer a full set of services to corporate customers. They've expanded from package delivery to worldwide logistics services—managing planes, trains, ships, and trucks in the process.

In every service industry, midsize, single-country companies are at an increasing disadvantage. Being big in the United States or Japan is no longer good enough. As ever-bigger corporations look to reduce the number of transactions and the problem of sorting out who is responsible for what, they want partners that can relive them of that burden. So, to gain instant breadth, service industries are following quickly in the mergers and acquisitions boom.

TO SUM UP

Striving to be what we term an oligonomy is not a new phenomenon, but it is a rapidly accelerating one. All of the frantic deal making of the past decade is an attempt not only to create oligopolies, but also to create oligopsonies. Only by protecting themselves in both directions can companies feel secure.

A few decades ago, in many sectors of our economy, there were lots of small, local, and regional companies at every level in the supply chain. There were lots of toy manufacturers, toy wholesalers, and toy retailers; lots of small food manufacturers, food brokers, and supermarket chains; lots of small stationery stores served by lots of distributors buying from many different vendors. But as one level in each market segment gets rolled up by a few dominant players, pressure is strong on other levels in the same supply chain to consolidate as well. This consolidation is necessary to be able to contend with both the companies they supply or serve and the companies that supply and serve them. The best answer to the problem of negotiating with an oligopoly is to become part of an oligopsony. The best answer to the problem of negotiating with an oligopsony is to become part of an oligopoly.

In this way, the rise to predominance of Best Buy and Circuit City, of Wal-Mart and Target, of Tyson and Cargill, eventually forces consolidation up and down the line. You want to get the contract with McDonald's for napkins? You'd better be big and operate nationwide. You want to handle public relations for Merck & Company? You'd better cover the world and have the resources to put a crack team together to limit the damage from a crisis like Vioxx. As companies get bigger, the companies that serve them must get bigger as well or lose out. A frenzy of mergers and acquisitions at every level is the result.

3 / Grow or Die

ALL BUSINESSES ARE EAGER TO GROW. In particular, all public corporations, those with shareholders, are under constant pressure to grow. Why can't everybody be happy with the status quo?

The answer may be obvious to many readers, but I know from conversations with intelligent people that many haven't really thought these ideas through. Furthermore, much of the writing in the business pages that tries to explain corporate moves seems to ignore the motivations for company growth and how they affect the behavior of companies. Bear with me while I explain the basics.

RETURN TO INVESTORS

All publicly held companies have as their main purpose a return to their investors. The firm may be nominally in the business of delivering packages, manufacturing automobiles, or accounting, but, in the deepest sense, their business is increasing the wealth of its stockholders.

There are two standard ways for public companies to reach that goal: either by returning cash payments to stockholders (dividends) or by increasing stock prices. Of course, many companies combine both approaches, but we will treat them here as separate paths.

The dividend path is usually pursued by companies in mature, steady businesses, where the opportunities for growth are limited but the cash flow is good and reliable and the risk is low. Stockholders are kept happy because they receive regular quarterly payments. The classic examples of this approach include utilities and some consumer products, such as food and tobacco. The pressure on such companies is great to keep the dividend steady, in spite of fluctuations in the business cycle or the cost of raw materials.

For all other companies, the price of each individual stock reflects its potential future prospects—that is, the hope that each buyer will be able to sell the stock for a higher price than they paid for it. That stock price involves not so much an assessment of the current value of the company and its assets, but a speculation on its future growth (or shrinkage). In this way, (new) companies that lose money still can experience rising stock prices, if the perception is that in the near future they will make money.

The managers of such companies are under enormous pressure to ensure steady and regular increases in the perceived value of the company. Wall Street analysts predict the expected financial results for the next quarter. Executives' and managers' jobs depend, to a great extent, on their ability to meet or surpass these goals. This can lead to major temptations, to fudging the numbers, and even to fraud (as at Enron, WorldCom, and elsewhere). In all companies, such expectations produce an exaggerated concern for short-term results.

The way for the stock price to rise is for the company to grow, and this growth can occur in two basic ways: in terms of *net income* (profit) or in terms of *gross income* (revenue). In the best scenario, you do both.

GROWING NET INCOME

Net income growth normally comes through three factors: cost-cutting, higher prices, and productivity gains. In other words, if you are running a steel company, you can increase net income (without selling more steel) in the following ways:

- Paying your employees less (cost-cutting)
- Finding cheaper raw materials (cost-cutting)
- Subcontracting nonprofitable work (cost-cutting)
- Charging more to your current customers (higher prices)
- Adjusting operations to favor higher-profit products (higher prices)
- Instituting a quality management program (productivity gains)
- Buying more efficient equipment (productivity gains)
- Reducing inventories through a just-in-time delivery program (productivity gains and cost-cutting)
- Selling off low-margin operations (probably all three, plus an inflow of cash)

And so on. These are issues that every executive deals with on an ongoing basis. They all have their risks. For example, charging more to current customers may lose their business to competitors, and buying cheaper raw materials may lower the quality of your product and eventually drive away customers.

GROWING GROSS INCOME

Gross income growth can be achieved in several ways: taking market share from the competition, selling new products and services, or opening new markets.

For example, at our same fictional steel mill you may increase gross income in the following ways:

- Beefing up your marketing effort (taking market share)
- Hiring top salespeople away from the competition (taking market share)
- Beating the prices of the competition (taking market share)
- Expanding from making bar steel into sheet steel (selling new products)
- Expanding the product list to include new alloys (selling new products)
- Finding customers in other regions, even other countries (opening new markets)
- Acquiring another company (opening new markets and/or selling new products)

Expanding gross income is inherently more risky in the long run than cutting costs and instituting productivity gains. All of the steps outlined above involve increases in spending, usually dramatic ones. While the expectation is that net income will increase eventually based on gross income increases, there is almost always a lag. That lag is caused by the added resources and increased spending that are necessary to expand, and it can take years to recoup the expenditure of expansion. Meanwhile, net income in the current quarter will certainly take a hit.

THE LURE OF MERGERS AND ACQUISITIONS

So here's the critical part: The easiest way to add to gross income is through mergers and acquisitions (M&As).

Buying an established business with developed products and markets is a lot easier than focusing on internal innovation or better business processes, as important as they are. Many companies add 30 percent, 50 percent, even 100 percent to the gross income line simply by making a strategic purchase.

The immediate effect of an acquisition on net income is usually negative. Cash reserves are swallowed up; debt is loaded on, and more stock is issued, diluting the value of each current share. In addition, key managers are overworked, others leave, familiar methods change, and morale is shaky, all factors trending to lower productivity. That is why most acquisitions cause an immediate drop in the stock price of the buyer. It's also why the business press badmouths almost every deal when it is announced.[1]

In truth, the pressure to grow at any cost can lead to foolish acquisitions. The folly of those deals may not be apparent for years. It is also true that growth can have side benefits (including a bigger voice in public policy and a stronger bargaining position with suppliers and customers) that can outweigh the immediate loss in income.

The mercilessness of the market is such that even when a company has grown in any given year, and done a good job in integrating acquisitions and cutting costs, there is always next year. At some point for every successful company, the "what have you done for me lately?" question comes up. Management is under pressure to grow again, and any rise in stock price from a year ago is ancient history.

A decrease in the rate of growth is also seen as a problem. When a successful company grows by a mere 5 percent per year in terms of gross income, rather than the predicted 10 percent, that slip is seen as a failure. Of course, this year's growth is often based on a higher starting figure than last year's. That scenario creates another reason to grow by acquisition, a quick fix for lagging growth.

At some point, growth in gross income has to translate into growth in net income. That day can be put off, but it cannot be avoided. Until then, new acquisitions can cover low or negative growth.[2]

WAYS TO GROW

Looking at the pressure to grow from a slightly different angle, as I see it, companies can grow in the following three basic ways:

- Organic growth (continuing to do what you're good at)
- Vertical expansion (buying up or down the supply chain)
- Horizontal expansion (buying into new business segments)

Organic Growth

The old-fashioned way for companies to grow is through internal growth. That's how, for example, McDonald's grew into its remarkable predominance. The company started with a single hamburger joint, added a few more, perfected a menu and a way of doing business, then started opening new stores in ever-expanding geographic areas. It added new food products until it had a full menu, even a breakfast menu. It expanded its hours. It honed its marketing and its managerial skills and its training for franchisees. It even expanded internationally and adapted to local tastes from France to Japan. But through it all, it remained almost totally the same company in terms of its business segment. In fact, when it has bought other kinds of franchises even within its narrow fast food segment (such as Boston Market and Chipotle Mexican Grill), it later gave up on them and went back to what it knew best (burgers and fries).

Likewise, Southwest Airlines started with a few routes and a few planes, perfected its way of doing business, and continued growing by expanding that model. It is now the #3 airline in the world in terms of passengers carried. This was done with minimal acquisitions or takeovers.[3]

Many companies manage to survive the first rough years by using a combination of innovation, hard work, and luck. Many fail; some succeed. Most compete with other small companies offering the same product or service and, through better location, superior sales and marketing, or great customer service, manage to build market share and thus survive.

But the organic growth approach has its risks as well. Such companies are vulnerable to a radical change in the market or an insuperable advantage from a competitor. The ground is littered with companies that were trapped in a dying or suddenly unprofitable area. For every McDonald's, there are several Burger Chefs that could not adapt. For every Southwest Airline, there's a Midway Airline.

The Vertical Dilemma

Companies often expand vertically by buying out companies involved in other layers of the same market. As we read in Chapter 2, industry segments work on several layers:

- In the DVD market, some companies own the content (the film studios), some manufacture the DVDs, others distribute the DVDs, and yet others sell or rent the DVDs at the retail level.
- In the beverage industry, some companies own the brand and the recipe, others bottle the products locally, and yet others sell retail (stores or restaurants).
- In the steel industry, some companies mine the iron-ore, some convert the ore to steel, others convert the steel into usable components (pipe, auto parts), and yet others (in some cases) buy the parts and assemble them.
- In the television industry, studios produce the shows, networks offer them, and local affiliate stations, or cable or satellite companies that carry the cable networks, show them.

When a company expands vertically, it takes over several of those intermediate levels. The objective is to maximize control, to no longer be at the mercy of some other company that has its own conflicting interests.

The consequence is usually increased control, but also increased risk. The risk comes in part from the pressure to use internal resources, when more effective or less costly alternatives are available on the outside. For example, an in-house print and design department is something many companies acquire or build, thinking they can get better response and lower costs from an internal operation. But such in-house operations are often dropped at a later date, because the wasted capacity and lack of competitive motivation may mean reduced service and greater expense.

Large companies often decide to spin off such acquired extensions because the pluses of cutting out the middleman are outweighed by the minuses of running yet another kind of unrelated business. In fact, there's a constant tension between the urge to vertically integrate and the desire to go in the other direction. In general, the tide has been running against vertical integration.

Nevertheless, such vertical integration persists, including in the following examples:

- Coca-Cola and PepsiCo have, over the last decade, steadily bought out independent bottlers that carry their brands.
- Large food companies like Kraft and General Mills increasingly deal directly with retailers, delivering producers directly to the food retailers, bypassing food brokers, and setting up their own truck distribution and warehousing systems.
- Supermarket chains and Wal-Mart have built large warehouse facilities to handle their own distribution direct from the manufacturer, thus squeezing food brokers from the other end.
- TV networks are more and more producing their own shows in their own studios, rather than buying shows from independent producers. They own many of the individual broadcast stations in big markets. Time Warner owns cable systems, and Fox (News Corp) owns its U.S. satellite system. Meanwhile, a cable company like Comcast is getting more and more into the business of producing shows and developing new cable channels.
- British plumbing supplier Wolseley PLC (the world's #1 plumbing and heating supplies manufacturer) has made more than a dozen acquisitions per year over the past decade. The acquisitions are up the supply chain (manufacturers of specialty plumbing products) and down the supply chain (small localized plumbing and heating supply firms in Europe and North America).

However, these examples of vertical integration are offset by many cases with opposite results. The disadvantages of vertical integration are well documented. It limits the company's flexibility by tying down capital and resources, making it harder to expand to new markets or adopt new business methods. It increases risk by further exposing the company to the ups and downs of the business cycle. Plus it allows companies to lose focus on so-called core competencies.

That's why, for example, the following companies sold off some of their operations:

- General Motors in 1999 spun off its Delphi auto parts division and Ford in 2000 followed suit by spinning off Visteon Automotive Systems, its auto parts supplier.
- Taiwanese cell phone maker BenQ spun off its manufacturing operations in 2005, electing to become a design, coordination, and sales organization only. Also in 2005, Canadian telephone equipment maker Nortel sold off its manufacturing operations to Flextronics.
- A large number of retail operations have sold off their in-house credit operations, including Sears (2003), Home Depot (2003), the Dillard

department store chain (2004), Circuit City (2004), the Belk department store chain (2005), and the newly merged May-Federated Department Store chain (2005). In each case, the buyer was a company specializing in credit card management.

That's not even to mention the constant process of outsourcing to other companies noncore operations from sales fulfillment to janitorial services. And companies are also sending tasks offshore to Third World countries while closing operations in the United States, whether in drug manufacturing and testing, staffing computer help desks, or even preparing tax returns.

Horizontal Expansion

While some companies like McDonald's stick to what they know best and keep improving it, and others try to gain more control of their whole supply chain, many other companies decide that they want to expand to other business areas. One reason for this preference may be that the executives believe the company has expertise that can be applied in a similar field. Another key motivator is the fear of being stuck in a declining or static business segment. Expansion can come through simply starting new departments and staffing them, but it is often achieved through M&As.

Here are some examples:

- Federal Express (FedEx) started by delivering small overnight packages by air. United Parcel Service (UPS) started by delivering larger packages by ground, normally within several days. Both companies expanded into each others' prime territory, as they realized that their skills carried over to an expanded role. UPS in the late 1990s got into overnight delivery (FedEx's specialty), while at the same time FedEx moved into land-based parcel delivery (UPS's forte). Now, both companies are expanding into the expediting business, helping large corporations manage the movement of raw materials and packaged goods in gross. Furthermore, UPS bought Mail Boxes Etc. to move into the business services sector. FedEx came back with the even more dramatic purchase of Kinko's, the copy and office services chain. These moves gave both companies an expanded retail presence in a related, but quite different, business.
- In 2001, Tyson, the #1 U.S. chicken producer, got into the beef and pork industry in a big way by acquiring IBP, #1 in beef and #2 in pork. In the same way, Smithfield Foods, the #1 pork producer, bought Farmland Beef in 2003, making it the #4 beef packer.
- In 2005, Cisco, the #1 supplier of network routers and switches, bought Scientific Atlanta, the leading supplier of set-top boxes for television users, used for distribution of video and other high-speed applications. This was a similar market with a common theme (high-speed

communications), but it also marked a move by Cisco to broaden itself into a new area with more potential for growth than its own maturing market.

- In 2001, Microsoft got into the accounting software business by acquiring Great Plains Software, the leading provider of midsize business accounting software.

Horizontal expansion, like vertical expansion, can be a mistake. In many cases, what looks like a logical expansion turns out to be nothing of the kind. Note the following examples:

- In 1998, Citibank merged with Travelers Insurance to form Citigroup. The idea was to sell insurance to their banking customers. In fact, it was the first company allowed to do so since the 1930s—the company was instrumental in having the law changed (the Glass-Stegal bill) to allow for the merger. But the insurance businesses dragged down the stock price. Citigroup spun off the Travelers Property Casualty units in 2004—Travelers later merged with St. Paul Companies, another insurance company. In 2005, Citigroup sold its life insurance and annuities underwriting business to MetLife. Underwriting insurance worked at a different speed than the banking world, and the move to horizontal expansion was abandoned by Citigroup.
- In 2006, the #3 U.S. movie rental company Movie Gallery outbid #1 Blockbuster to buy the #2 chain, Hollywood Video, for $1.25 billion. The deal gave Movie Gallery a total of 4,600 outlets across North America, even as the retail movie rental business is in rapid decline. Moreover, sales at Hollywood Video stores are declining enough to drag down the more profitable Movie Gallery stores.[4] As movie studios and high-speed Internet providers gear up (finally) for digital delivery, the weakening rental business could be nearing the edge of a cliff.
- PepsiCo went into the restaurant business by buying Taco Bell (1976), Pizza Hut (1977), and KFC (1986). PepsiCo did well in expanding all three brands, with KFC and Pizza Hut becoming global brands. But the rate of return for the restaurants moved at a different pace than PepsiCo's drinks and snacks businesses. In 1997, PepsiCo spun off the restaurants as Tricon Global Restaurants, which changed its name to YUM! Brands (the exclamation point is indeed part of the name). The spin-off was a great deal for PepsiCo shareholders, and PepsiCo had done very well for itself in investment terms. Operationally, however, the restaurants were not a good fit.

BUYING RIVALS

The most common kind of horizontal expansion is buying a major direct rival with a somewhat different clientele, another region of coverage, or certain products and services that you lack and cannot easily create. It's a smart move, and even better, it takes a competitor out of the market, allowing for further oligopolization.

These deals are likelier to succeed than random company extensions because the buyers are familiar with the business of the company they buy. Because they have been competing with these companies, they may already know the executives and the salespeople, and they certainly know the products and services. For that reason, the acquisition of a rival is less of a roll of the dice than more distant acquisitions.

Examples include the following:

- Bank of America bought Fleet Bank in 2003. Like hundreds of other bank deals over the last ten years, the two companies were pretty similar in operation, ranging from checking accounts to commercial loans, credit cards, and investment management. They simply had different geographic distribution, and Fleet Bank (itself the result of a long series of M&As among New England banks) had a leading regional position. Bank of America, with major operations in much of the country, had little New England presence. The new company is just a bigger version of the two existing companies (and both banks were built from a series of mergers with other banks).
- In 2005, Time Warner Cable and Comcast carved up the cable TV assets of the Adelphia Communications after that company went out of business.
- In 2006, Coors Brewing Company, the #3 U.S. brewing company, bought Molson Brewing, the #1 brewery in Canada. While there is some difference in their beers (and Molson's is sold as a "semi-premium" import in the United States), the two companies sell similar products through similar outlets and similar marketing campaigns. For Coors, the deal was an attempt to keep up with expanding international beer companies like SABMiller (owner of the #2 U.S. beer brand Miller) and InBev (which owns Canada's #2 brewer Labatt.)
- In 2006, Maytag bought Whirlpool. The two American appliance giants (#1 and #2, respectively) have an almost identical range of products (washers, dryers, ovens, stove tops, refrigerators, and so on). In the United States, they are each other's biggest (sometimes only) competitor throughout much of their lines. The two deal with the same retailers and appeal to the same customers.

Adjacencies

The practice of the modern multinational has been to expand horizontally in markets that are adjacent to, or parallel with, the ones they already own. This means buying a company where your already established expertise, connections, and muscle can be used to foster real growth.

One example of adjacent buying is the 2005 purchase of Gillette by Procter & Gamble. This may be the ideal adjacent purchase. Most of Procter & Gamble's retailers were the same as Gillette's retailers, and there is almost no overlap in products. P&G specialized in health and beauty products for women, while Gillette specialized in men's toiletries. There was minimal overlap in their product lines, and together they were an even more formidable force.

Another case is that of LVMH, which in 1986 brought together three seemingly incompatible products from Louis Vuitton (luggage), Moët et Chandon (champagne), and Hennessy (high-end brandy). The three companies and product lines appealed to the same audience, people who have a taste for luxury and the money to spend on it. The company has since acquired a list of product lines that are equally incompatible in everything but their intended target audiences: prestige watches (TAG Heuer, Zenith International), fashion (Christian Dior, Givenchy, Donna Karan, Emilio Pucci), perfume (Guerlain), fountain pens (OMAS), and retail outlets (La Samaritaine, Sephora). Most of these brands were acquired methodically over the past twenty years, one by one. They are a remarkable collection of adjacencies.

THE FEAR FACTOR BEHIND ACQUISITIONS

Mergers and acquisitions create stress in any industry in which they take place. Executives wonder whether their company will miss out on the dance by sitting on the sidelines. They worry whether they can survive when other rivals keep getting bigger. The acquisition scramble snowballs. In this way, consolidation breeds consolidation.

So M&As tend to come in waves. Some of this is related to external conditions, including the perceived value of the operations in a market segment or the loosening of antitrust rules. But a lot of it is based on anxiety.

Once a sector starts consolidating, other players feel the need to follow suit to maintain market power and to deny growth to others. After a few acquisitions, panic sets in and a feeding frenzy erupts. Now, most large companies are always exploring the chance to buy out other firms in their industry, but the segmentwide anxiety moves the deal making from the back to the front burner. M&As are contagious.[5]

For the potential acquirees, that panic time, with suitors bidding high, must look like the best time to cash in, since the buying panic sends prices up. And certainly, late buyers pay more than they might have if they had acted earlier.

ROLLING UP AN INDUSTRY

In an often-repeated scenario, a few M&As can trigger a flurry of buys that turns into a feeding frenzy. One big company matches another's acquisition, then the first company and others in the industry feel threatened and, boom, there's another acquisition. In a short time, the level of concentration in the industry surges as company after company is bought out.

The U.S. telephone industry has been rolled up thoroughly over the last decade, with one acquisition seemingly driving another, as companies tried to maintain their market positions. It has happened from top to bottom, in the traditional land-line operations, in cell phones, and in corporate telephone services, until only two major players remain (Verizon and the new AT&T), plus a few mid-size ones (Sprint Nextel and Qwest).

Something similar has happened in Latin America, where Mexico's Amercia Movil and Spain's Telefonica have now bought out most of the cell phone companies in every country. It happened in Europe, especially in Eastern Europe, where companies like U.K.-based Vodafone, Norway's Telenor, Spain's Telefonica, Sweden's Tele2, and others have been bidding up once-local providers from Albania to Poland.

Similar frenzies have consolidated breweries, banks, midsize oil companies, and mining companies. Anxiety at being left out has led, undoubtedly, to more than a few imprudent buys, in which the promised synergies weren't delivered.

SYNERGY AND ANTERGY

Every M&A touts the supposed synergies of the move. The word "synergy" is a kind of magic incantation that populates press releases.

Here are some random examples taken from the Web. We'll leave out the company names, as the releases essentially are interchangeable.

- "This is a strategic, transforming merger based on account acquisition synergies generated. . . ."
- "Post-acquisition synergies coupled with a high revenue growth rate will allow us to exceed our normal rate of return threshold."
- "In addition, we believe that the increased purchasing power from this acquisition will enable [company X] to achieve significant cost synergies while further leveraging our global manufacturing capability."

And, as a prime exhibit, a veritable banquet of business buzzwordese:

- "The synergies will reduce both cost of goods sold and operating expenses and primarily be generated by eliminating redundancies in internal programs, processes and employee positions, rationalizing facilities, leveraging higher manufacturing volumes to reduce supply chain costs, and streamlining procurement processes."

Of course, synergies do exist. As the quotes above assert, the ability to combine back-office operations, reduce staff, and buy cheaper can make a real difference to the future success of a company. The question is not whether there are synergies, but whether they justify the price and disruptiveness of any particular deal.

But all too often the predicted synergies fall short of projections. As one analyst notes, "Financiers call this phenomenon unrealized synergies and it's so prevalent that merger and acquisition announcements usually include disclaimer language along the lines of 'if all synergies are realized.' They rarely are."[6]

Spectacular failures are not just found in examples like the AOL–Time Warner merger or the French water company Vivendi's acquisition of Universal Studios. Ford's purchases of such companies as Jaguar, Land Rover, and Volvo were, in retrospect, big mistakes, as was General Motors' purchase of Saab, and Volkswagen's of Rolls Royce. (What was the attraction of these British and Swedish auto companies?) Compaq's takeover of minicomputer maker Digital Equipment was a poor decision as well. By contrast, HP's seemingly foolish acquisition of Compaq now looks like a smart move. The Tribune Company's acquisition of the *Los Angeles Times*, as it turns out, was a disastrous decision.

Aside from the big goofs, plenty of quieter acquisitions simply fail to deliver the goods. Sears bought the Lands' End mail order clothing retailer in 2002 to boost its sales; it didn't help. U.K.-based multinational wireless carrier Vodafone acquired J-Phone, Japan's #3 wireless carrier in 2002; in 2006, it sold it off as it lost customers and Vodafone failed to find economies of scale. French-based Suez Water (the #2 water utility operator in the world) bought American Nalco, the #1 maker of water treatment equipment, in 1999. A marriage made in heaven, right? By 2002, Suez sold off the company to private investors, apparently not having seen any hope of the expected return.

Well-known corporate consultant The McKinsey Group discovered that a shocking 70 percent of M&As fail to deliver the synergies promised at the time of the deal. "Our research indicates that this happens primarily because acquirers overestimate the synergies mergers yield and underestimate the costs they create."[7]

ULTERIOR MOTIVES

Of course, not all motivations for M&As have to do with the welfare of a business or the happiness of the stockholders. Many acquisitions are caused by the financial interests of the principals who engineer them.

Any merger or acquisition is a big payday for some insiders. There are the executives of the purchased company, who get sweetheart deals and cash in their options; the executives of the buying company, who can demand higher compensation for the expertise it takes to run an even bigger company; there are bankers, lawyers, and (often enough) insider traders.

According to a *New York Times* article, "Sometimes Investors Should Just Say No," a number of major stockholders (such as mutual fund company Putnam Investments) felt that a deal selling Providian Bank to Washington Mutual Bank severely undervalued Providian.[8] That issue came up especially since Bank of America was far more generous in buying Providian's close competitor MBNA a few months earlier, a similar deal for credit card assets.

The perception was that the executives and directors of Providian were more interested in lining their pockets than in enriching the stockholders. As the *Times* article reported,

> After all, the interests of executives in most mergers are not necessarily aligned with those of their companies' shareholders. Executives of the company being acquired hit the jackpot in these deals because their stock option grants, restricted shares and retirement plans turn into instant cash. If their companies remained independent, this largess would be accessible only over longer periods.[9]

The article enumerates the windfall that would hit Joseph Saunders, CEO of Providian, if the merger went through as structured, which included:

- 1.1 million shares of Providian in the form of options to be cashed in at once (over $19 million)
- Merger payments equal to three times his Providian salary
- A new, high-paying job at Washington Mutual (as president of the credit card division) at a hefty salary as long he wants it
- $2 million in new, restricted shares in Washington Mutual

The directors of Providian's board wouldn't be so richly rewarded, but they would be sent off with a nice payday as well.

The Providian case was not an isolated case. Bushels of cash are shaken loose with any such deal, all buried under transaction costs. The obvious conclusion is that these factors cannot help but get in the way of good decision making.

Another *New York Times* article, "No Wonder CEO's Love Those Mergers," notes that shareholders generally like to have their company acquired, as long as they reap a neat profit on their stocks, but executives like it even more, as they end up "truly, titanically, stuperfyingly rich."[10]

Among the more profitable (for executives) buyouts noted in the article are the following:

- The CEO of Caesars Entertainment, received over $26 million thanks to that company's acquisition by Harrah's (2004).
- The CEO of SouthTrust bank, took in $59 million in termination awards and an annual pension of $3.8 million from the acquisition by Wachovia Bank (2004).
- Anthem and WellPoint executives made an estimated $67 million in compensation for the merger of those two health care companies (2004).

With so many M&As, there are a lot of very rich unemployed execs. In addition to the big payouts, there are options, pensions, health care, and other perks to cushion their lamentable fate. Moreover, the company often pays all the onerous taxes incurred by the executives, as well as covers legal fees. The whole executive package, says the article, may constitute up to 8 percent of a merger's cost.

This usually passes in silence. As the *Times* article states, "Yet shareholders have no way to know about this in advance because it is hidden from view. The attitude seems to be, why bother the owners with chapter and verse on what the hired help will get?"[11]

In terms of deals running tens of billions of dollars, it can be argued that a few hundred million here or there are just crumbs off the table. But the issue is not whether executives get paid too much, but rather whether the lure of such large payoffs is a greater motivating factor than the oft-claimed synergies.

Disclosure regulations are lax, and only the interest of a few pension funds brings this stuff to light. Why wouldn't a company executive want his or her company to be taken over? Well, there is sheer ego.

Company CEOs, especially founders, are notoriously self-confident and addicted to growth—that's a requirement of the job. But once a business is established, the pursuit of becoming a Napoleon of industry is often part of the reason some companies want to grow ever bigger. Notorious examples of such megalomania include News Corp's Rupert Murdoch, who desired to build a hereditary global empire, and Oracle's Lawrence Ellison, whose single-minded pursuit of rival PeopleSoft became a point of personal fulfillment. Enron and Vivendi were companies where hubris in the executive was a clear motivator for disastrous acquisitions. The pride at being the CEO of a $1 billion company rather than a $500 million company is certainly a major motivator beyond simply the extra cash.

GIN RUMMY

One way to look at the sequence of acquisitions is by analogy to the card game gin rummy. As playing card games other than poker and blackjack has suffered a long decline, I assume that many people under 40 have little or no knowledge of the game. So here's a description.

Basically, gin rummy (or gin) is a card game with two players. After initial cards are dealt, the play involves making "melds" and getting rid of "deadwood." Melds are combinations of three or more cards (either cards of the same value—say, deuces—or cards in the same suit that are in sequences— say, the king, queen, and jack of diamonds). You win the game by being able to lay down melds and having no cards left in your hand.

The play is a series of picking up cards and discarding them onto the discard pile. You discard what you judge to be deadwood, cards that don't fit into your potential melds. You can take a new card sight unseen from the deck, or you can pick up the top card on the discard pile.

Here's the analogy. Many companies are in a constant flurry of activity, acquiring and de-acquiring business units. Each pickup is trumpeted as the perfect fit to existing lines of business, a business meld. Each discard is obviously

The Company Wants . . .

In this book, as in all business writing, the problem of how to write about a company's actions and intentions leads to shortcut expressions that don't represent reality. Let me illustrate with a number of random quotes off the Web, most from business magazines or business sections of newspapers:

- "The company wanted to cross sell products across business unit product lines."
- "What it all comes down to is that Microsoft intends to dominate every market that it contacts."
- "Apple doesn't want music consumers to have freedom of portability."
- "At the simplest level, he says, it is because GE wants to be known as a good company."
- "Cargill would like to control the trade in food and to make larger profits by buying cheaply from farmers."
- "Looking at this acquisition on the surface, IBM has always wanted a piece of the retail market."
- "Known for its thriftiness, Disney hates being made to look like a typical money-burning Hollywood studio."

In all of these quotes, companies are presented as having wills of their own. It's shorthand, of course, pointing at the management at the companies cited. We all understand that, or do we?

It is easy to slip from such statements to a personification of companies as beings with intrinsic desires and tastes. In the IBM example above, the use of "always wanted" compounds this, making it seem like a company has a continued will over time, in spite of changes in management. And people see companies as having human characteristics, such as greed, aggression, or friendliness.

Much less personification is involved when we write something like "IBM plans" or "Microsoft says," in that these companies do have planning departments or spokespeople. But wanting and hating are human traits, and it's easy to think of big companies as self-willed Titans—just Google the phrases "hates God" or "hates America" and you'll find a good number of corporations supposedly bedeviled with these emotions.

On a side note, the British use of the corporate plural ("BP are" or "HSBC seek") comes closer to the mark, implying that a group of people are involved, not a monolith, symbolic person. And part of this has to do with the U.S. constitutional law fiction that corporations are "persons," having the 14th Amendment rights of individuals—although that's a topic for another book.

It's easy to use shorthand (attentive readers will find me doing it at times in this volume). But companies do not have wills independent of those of their top management, and with every mention of a company's intentions, the "top management of the company" is implied.

But even that is too simplistic. The individuals who make up the management of a company have all kinds of motives that are incidental to what corporate goals might be. Self-aggrandizement (vanity), filling their pockets (greed), and keeping jobs (fear) are all major motivators.

Furthermore, more often than not, executives are thinking about the next quarter or the next year. Having a long-term strategy, at least in publicly held firms, is all very well, but such a strategy cannot come at too big a short-term price.

Chances are that both management and stockholders will substantially change over a five-year period. Private equity investors may have the patience to wait three or four years to reap a long-term profit, but even they have their limits. Only tightly held companies can afford a longer time frame to achieve their plans and desires.

We have to watch ourselves from dwelling too much on long-term strategy in place of short-term gains, especially in public companies. Obviously, all short-term moves have long-term consequences, but most of the applied wishing comes from stressed-out executives worried about getting through the next few quarters, not a company building a legacy for itself. The legacy, when it comes, is built on lots of short-term decisions (or nondecisions) by specific people. Companies are not the agents, in the sense of conscious wills, executives are.

---

considered deadwood, a drag on profits and not organic to company success. The objective is a winning hand (although with companies the game never really ends).

The parallels are strong, but in one specific area they are deficient. Gin rummy players are limited to seven cards, and they can't pick up cards that were discarded earlier in the game. But there is another game in the rummy family that comes closer to the strategies of big acquirers. Canasta, which originated in South America and was incredibly popular in the United States in the middle of the last century, is gin rummy squared.[12] It starts with a much bigger deck, including two standard fifty-two-card decks and four added jokers. Players can pick up one card off the discard pile or can take the whole pile, often allowing them to have enormous hands with the ability to work on large melds. Canasta is a far wilder game than gin rummy, and each hand is likely to last for a long time.

We frequently see one company acquire another, and after the deal is done, sell off (discard) divisions or brands that do not fit into the core business activities of the acquirer. That, for example, fits the recent case of newspaper publisher McClatchy Publishing, which bought out rival Knight Ridder in 2006, only to retain those papers (small regional ones) that fit its business model and sell off all the others (including the *Philadelphia Inquirer* and the *Miami Herald*).

Similarly, in 2000, drug giant Pfizer purchased its pharmaceutical rival Warner-Lambert. With the purchase, Pfizer also picked up several companies that Warner-Lambert had accumulated over the years. These included Adams Gum (#2 in the world, with such brands as Dentyne, Chiclets, and Trident) and Schick-Wilkinson Sword razors (the #2 razor seller in the world). Pfizer decided that these businesses, however successful, were not adjacent enough to their drug business, and they discarded (sold) them. In 2002, Cadbury Schweppes judged that Adams Gum fit in nicely with existing candy sales, where the Adams products could be sold by the same salesmen to the same retailers and delivered by the same trucks. They would even sit adjacent on the shelves—a great pickup.

In 2003, Pfizer discarded Schick-Wilkinson, which was picked up by battery maker Energizer Holdings. Although these products would not sit on adjacent shelves, they are sold through the same stores (pharmacies, supermarkets, and convenience stores) and could be delivered by the same trucks. More important, it would allow Energizer to compete on a second front with rival Gillette, whose Duracell batteries gained an advantage from its association with the best-selling shaving equipment.

Likewise, companies spend enormous amounts of time and energy developing (mostly through acquisitions) a new division, and then decide that they'd rather spin off or sell the division. For example, radio/billboard company Clear Channel took great pains to dominate the live pop music concert business, buying many smaller local companies and their concert sites, and working out long-term agreements with exclusive producer rights at other venues. In 2005, it spun off the business as a new company called Live Nation, seeking to boost revenue and, perhaps, reduce conflicting motivations. Clear Channel management realized that synergies were, in the end, elusive and the antitrust risks great.

TO SUM UP

Company executives want to grow for a variety of reasons, and greed is a major one. But even more important is fear. Constant expansion, year over year, whether in gross or net income, is the only way to keep investors happy. And all investors keep ratcheting up the base level for judging company growth. Results from last year are history; from two years ago, ancient history. It's possible to see most M&As as an attempt to buy a little more time. (Privately held companies can afford a longer-term view, but the expectations of growth are ultimately the same.)

Fear also figures in when loss of market share and market position are factored in. When some companies in an industry are bulking up, the rival companies are under enormous pressure to get bigger as well, if only to hold their place and not be swallowed up in turn.

In this atmosphere of fear, the complete rationality of many deals is, to say the least, uncertain. Every major acquisition is a combination of investment and wager. Talk of synergy and complementary operations can't hide the fact that in an active M&A market few bargains are overlooked by other companies. Many deals are the result of an auction, and the winner (as in many auctions) can easily lose sight of its original intentions in the excitement of beating its rivals.

Another source of fear for all company stakeholders is that it will suddenly become obsolete, that it will be tripped up by a new technology, a new fashion, or a new way of doing business that others have mastered and exploited. That fear of missing the boat, of being behind the innovation curve, is yet another reason that companies aggressively buy others.

4 / Disruption and Innovation

THE BERKELEY-BASED POWERBAR COMPANY was founded in 1986 by a former Canadian Olympic marathoner and his nutritionist wife, the kind of high-energy business neophytes that *Inc.* magazine likes to celebrate. By 1999, the firm had reached sales of over $135 million, taking a specialized and minor product type, the nutrition bar, and turning it into a market phenomenon.

The company was a classic case of a gutsy entrepreneur with a great idea who built a new category and a new business at the same time. The closest analogy is Gatorade, formulated by doctors at the University of Florida, and bought by Quaker in 1983.[1] Like Gatorade, PowerBar was yet another breakthrough product intended for athletes that spread to a far wider audience.

According to an interview with PowerBar founder Brian Maxwell, his company was aiming ever higher. "From a strategic standpoint, we've had some aggressive goals such as growing by 30% a year.... We've been growing very rapidly. We saw there were opportunities out there to grow into a $1 billion to $2 billion business, but we needed the resources of a global partner."[2]

As with many smaller businesses, the struggle to hold and expand shelf space in retail stores, ensure on-time distribution, and conduct face-to-face negotiations with large chains was starting to swamp the company by the year 2000. There was no way such a small company could grow so fast, and other companies, noticing PowerBar's success, were starting to aggressively release new products. A white knight was urgently needed. And that's where Nestlé, already serving most of the same retailers PowerBar wanted to reach, both domestically and globally, stepped in.[3]

In many ways, Nestlé was a perfect fit. It had a large presence in supermarkets and convenience stores, and it could effortlessly demand space for its products. It had a full force of experienced salespeople out on the street. It was a master of distribution, inventory management, and marketing. It had leverage in buying raw materials and services like printing and transport. It had a global presence with the money to invest in a worldwide campaign. For Nestlé, too, it was a great deal—a product similar to the candy bars that made up one of its main profit centers, yet a new and relatively uncontested market with higher markups.[4]

How is Nestlé doing with PowerBar? Nestlé doesn't release separate numbers, but it appears that the investment was a good one. In the nutrition bar arena, the big competitors are Kraft (Balance Bar), Clif (Luna, Clif Bar), and Unilever (SlimFast). There are various claims for PowerBar's market share, but it continues to be the market leader in a market that has grown rapidly. It has created a worldwide presence by creating new markets for nutrition bars from Taiwan to Brazil and from Germany to Australia. It keeps adding new Power-Bar products, now including a branded set of sports drinks. PowerBar has been proven to be a strong addition to Nestlé's product mix.

The PowerBar story has been repeated again and again. Market-dominating companies like Nestlé are increasingly acquisition machines. For many companies, buying other companies, often small start-ups, has become a major engine of expansion—often far more successful than the company's own product development efforts. This frenzy of acquisition is rooted in dread—the fear of being outflanked by someone else's innovation.

LONELY AT THE TOP OF THE MARKET

As powerful as oligopolies (and oligopsonies) often are, they can't rely on their dominant positions. At least from management's point of view, the dominating issue is less often greed than fear—fear of the investors, fear of the competition, and above all, fear of *disruption*.

The annals of business are full of examples of major companies that were done in by complacency. And the problem was often not in the struggle against traditional big rivals, but rather by the appearance of smaller upstarts who have gotten in front of new ideas, trends, and techniques and outflanked the dominant position of big companies.

At one time perhaps, companies could easily get cozy as long as they kept their "friendly enemies" at bay. But the exhortations of business gurus like Tom Peters (*Reimagine: Business Excellence in a Disruptive Age!*[5]), Henry Mintzberg (*Managers Not MBAs*[6]), and John P. Kotter (*Leading Change*[7]) have made fighting complacency a central issue. Even more unavoidable are the lessons in the demise of once top-of-the-world companies as diverse as Bethlehem Steel, Polaroid, Digital Equipment, Wang Laboratories, and TWA. All this can make sane chief executives look nervously about for the little guy who might upset the apple cart, the seemingly trivial technological advance that might make their operations into dinosaurs, or the "unrelated" social trend that is about to gain mass and roll over them.

The way in which industries were shaken up by innovators was laid out by the Austrian-Czech economist Joseph Schumpeter (1883–1950), who discussed the "process of industrial mutation—if I may use that biological term—that incessantly revolutionizes the economic structure *from within*, incessantly destroying the old one, incessantly creating a new one."[8] He called this process *creative destruction*.

Needless to say, this destruction is a painful process for many, an enormous boon for others. Most vulnerable are the comfortable and complacent companies who live off past innovations and commanding market positions. In the survival-of-the-fittest companies, it is often hardest for the mastodon to adapt to rapid changes in the market.

DISRUPTIVE INNOVATION

Furthermore, Schumpeter's follow-up idea is that innovation is the engine of business cycles and that disruption of the ongoing course of the economy, in turn, stimulates more innovation, then more disruption. The ideas of "disruptive innovation" and "creative destruction" resonate ever more in our time as the pace of change accelerates and as businesses are utterly transformed not in decades, but in years.

In the 1990s, Kodak executives came up with a plan to deal with the gradual loss of its film business to digital photography, but almost no one inside or outside the company could see how fast the move to digital would pull out the rug from under Kodak or how difficult it would be to avoid the crash. Likewise, no company or union in the early 1990s foresaw how fast the trade barriers with China, India, and other countries would come down and how this would affect them, for better or for worse.

There is little doubt that we live in a time of major disruption and destruction. Almost every week, a time-honored firm bites the dust through acquisition or simple bankruptcy. At the same time, recently ascendant hot shots in information technology, biotech, and retailing get swallowed up one after another.

All this movement in the market shows that the creation of oligopolies and oligopsonies is a constant process, not a one-time task. These are not inherently stable market states, so companies who want to preserve their market domination cannot afford to rest. In fact, their very success can make them vulnerable.

Incremental and Disruptive Innovations

The word innovation is a rather vague term. It can be used for everything from the invention of the Internet to the invention of four-track razor blades to replace mere three-track models. It seems clear that the latter is not the innovation that stimulates creative destruction.

Many business theorists now make a distinction between incremental innovations and disruptive innovations. *Incremental*, or *sustaining, innovations* are those that improve an existing product or service by upgrading performance, extending features, or adapting to different uses. The transition from old single-track razors to a four-track shaving Nirvana has been carried forth by a set of many small and incremental innovations, no matter how "revolutionary" the marketers claim every feature upgrade to be. *Disruptive innovations*, on the other hand, redefine a product or service and how it is used or understood. The original Gillette invention of the disposable safety razor blade in 1901 was a disruptive innovation, one that changed the nature of a daily activity for almost all men (and many women) and totally restructured the economics of the razor industry and the barbering profession.

Incremental innovation is an ongoing process in most industries, necessary to hold on to (or expand) market share. Its nature is evolutionary in the sense that it involves generation after generation of adaptations—to competition, to changed market environments, to new political and economic conditions, and to improved technology. Companies that don't innovate in this way soon fade away. At a minimum, you have to regularly come out with a "new, improved" version of your product or service (unless you are selling 20-year-old Scotch or Persian carpets).

One aspect of incremental innovation is seen in the doctrine of "continuous improvement." That idea has its origins in the time-and-motion studies of American efficiency expert Frederick Winslow Taylor.[9] It has its flowering in the Japanese manufacturing doctrine of Kaizen and the quality management ideas now adopted by most companies in the world. Continuous improvement involves constantly finding small advantages in work processes, often simple steps that add up to major improvements, not only in manufacturing efficiency but also in the end result.

Take as an example the constant improvement found in Toyota automobiles. The amazing evolution of Toyota (and Honda) cars from perceived "toys" to market beaters is in their corporatewide attention to detail. Each new year's release of Camrys and Accords is improved in small ways in almost every aspect, from fuel efficiency and engine reliability to the look and feel of the controls and the seats. Both companies have grown through the mastery of improving what exists, while many rivals have not kept pace.

The Power of Disruptive Innovation

The scenario for disruption goes something like this:

- A company dominates its market by dominance in manufacturing, marketing, or service. It has achieved some form of equilibrium with its main competitors, which it resembles as they resemble it in turn.
- An individual or a small group makes an exciting industry breakthrough. If they go to the big company with the idea (and they may already be employees), they leave unheeded. The process is unproven, the return is unlikely, and the demand isn't there. Why should a multibillion dollar company look at some crazy outside idea when they can make a few million through a new accounting maneuver,

outsourcing manufacturing, or by releasing a new improved version of their product?

- The new company goes out and scrapes up the money to test the concepts. In the majority of cases, there's little or nothing there. Once in a while, there is something that not only works, but that also has a profitable market and perhaps is even patentable. Even at this stage, the big company is pooh-poohing the idea.
- In even rarer cases, the product (or service) invented causes a real revolution, a tipping-point moment. Suddenly, everyone seems to start using the service or buying the product. The old company, too slow to turn, sees its revenue dropping, perhaps even its business going away.

A true Horatio Alger story, except that Alger never dwelt on the majority of clever entrepreneurs who see their mortgages, retirement savings, and ideas go up in smoke. Disruptive innovation is risky business. But when it succeeds, it can be well worth the gamble.

This disruptive story is the plot of classic business sagas. For example, Japanese electronics companies in the 1960s and 1970s jumped on transistors and solid-state electronic (albeit an American invention) in a way that RCA and Sylvania did not. Burroughs, Sperry, and Digital Equipment never quite adapted to the microcomputer (although IBM managed to be dragged into adopting it). Typesetting companies and their suppliers scoffed at the notion of doing page layout on those same "toy" computers, only to find themselves bankrupt in a few years.

PREPARING FOR DISRUPTION

The fact is that many big companies have learned the lessons that come with disruption and are more aware of the need to react to disruptive change. More than ever, most companies are aware that however dominant they might be in a market, circumstances can change and leave them behind. And because most markets are now global, not local or even national, companies are vulnerable to disruptive attack from increasingly unsuspected sources. But the hubris that allowed an underestimated Japanese television manufacturing industry to so easily take over the U.S. market is less common than it was. Even the Japanese are looking over their shoulders at the Koreans and Chinese, and it may soon be the case that Bucharest or Bangkok will be the source of the next big thing. Most company executives could be considered paranoid about competition, except that their fears are well-founded.

BIG COMPANIES AND INNOVATION

But big companies are innovative, aren't they? How else did they get to their current eminence and profitability?

BusinessWeek each year lists the top-100 most innovative companies. And almost all of those companies are among the biggest. The 2006 list is full of companies like Microsoft, Intel, Nike, Procter & Gamble, and Toyota.[10] All of the 100 companies on the list could be said to be intent on changing products and processes, but look at the kind of innovation going on at a Microsoft: an upgraded Xbox, an iPod wanna-be, and a late and not-very-exciting Windows upgrade or a minor add-on to Internet Explorer. Although Microsoft often makes successful products, it rarely, if ever, comes up with the original idea. Their "innovations" don't belong in the same ballpark as the truly disruptive innovations created by, for example, Google or Apple.

More surprising yet is Sony's thirteenth-place finish on the *BusinessWeek* list. The company, at least according to some observers, is running on empty in the innovation department.[11] Whatever *BusinessWeek* means by innovation, it's not (in most cases) breakthrough innovations. Also note Starbuck's inclusion at #9—could this be due to a new version of decaf-soymilk macchiato or to one of the hip lifestyle CDs they now sell?

Yes, these companies are all expert at making numerous incremental enhancements on lots of products and services. They keep improving business processes to cut costs and increase flexibility, but most of the established companies on the list don't make breakthrough changes.

Since innovation is hard to measure, some analysts see it in terms of patents accumulated. By this measure, companies like General Electric, NEC, Microsoft, and IBM are the most innovative, as their labs crank out patents like nobody's business. But (and we'll discuss this later) few of these could be classified as disruptive innovations, at least not when compared with the innovations from teeny companies like Netflix, Amazon, and (nonprofit) Wikipedia.

Drug Companies

After a major deal is made between drug companies, the claim is often made that bigger companies can innovate more because they have better combined research and development (R&D) resources and greater ability to get new products on the market. Thirty-eight major drug companies have merged since 1994, and one of the chief reasons cited for most of these mergers was building "lab synergies."[12] The reality, however, is that merged companies are less successful at innovation, at least in the pharmacy industry.

For example, GlaxoSmithKline, which is the #2 drug company in the world (after Pfizer), is the result of a series of mergers over the past decade. The main components of the current company include Swiss-based Glaxo, U.K.-based Burroughs Wellcome, and U.S.-based Smith, Kline French. The thought was that that they would create a new research and marketing powerhouse that could expedite getting a steady flow of new drugs on the market.

It's pretty clear, however, that the pace of innovation has slowed to a trickle. The company has produced only one major new drug a year, for the last few years, and the consensus is that it needs to introduce five a year to maintain profits, as its money-making older drugs like Paxil lose patent protection from generics. But that's not just GlaxoSmithKline's problem. According to a *New York Times* article, "Poor lab production is bedeviling almost every drug company. Across the industry, introductions of new drugs plummeted last year to 17 from a high of 53 in 1995, despite a near doubling in annual research spending to $22 billion."[13]

Of course, plenty of other reasons might contribute to a slowdown in new drug development. But the chief culprit has been the chaos caused by mergers, and its impact on lab scientists, who are constantly immersed in corporate politics. "The bureaucratic task of combining two companies became the sole chore for many top scientists, some of whom had to shuttle between continents, they said. That took a toll on research projects." As one researcher noted, "What ensued was an incredible number of arguments about who was doing what."[14] The result was multiyear-long demoralization that sucked the creativity out of the process of drug creation, a process that combines inspiration with systematic proof.

Smaller, creative firms merged to form slow-moving mastodons. It seems to reflect a change in attitude toward risk, a breakdown in communication, and a deeper politicization of the whole enterprise. It comes down to this: as companies get bigger and anxious to maintain the *status quo*, they rely less on flexibility and originality and more on brute market power. In many cases, "synergy" turns into lethargy, as too much depends on maintaining the status quo.

Innovators' Dilemmas

This difficulty in really innovating is one of the points of Clayton Christensen's landmark book, *The Innovator's Dilemma*.[15] The book shows how successful companies are far more likely to budget development dollars for extending already successful products and brands (low risk, almost certain return) rather than budget for truly new products (high risk, unlikely return). That's the nature of how institutions work, once they are established. For start-ups, rolling the dice is a way of life, and once in a while, there's a big payoff for the gamble. But Christensen shows how this process leaves established companies vulnerable to new thinking, new technology from outside.

Large companies tend toward stasis. It's difficult, as most management consultants have pointed out, to create an atmosphere of entrepreneurialism in an environment where you are likely to keep your job if you keep doing today pretty much what you were doing yesterday. For employees, it is a rational choice. Why risk making a big mistake when you can go on doing a slightly improved version of what you have always been doing? Tearing apart existing organizational structures risks hastening the demise of the business and, more immediately, the loss of a job.

In spite of all this awareness, big companies are inherently bad at creating disruptive innovation. Their investment is better repaid if they make evolutionary innovations, improving products for which they know they have a market.

Striving for disruption is just too risky. But oligopolies have learned that they have to move fast whenever there is a threat of disruption and they must use money and market power to keep the disrupters under their control. They obviously can't do this all the time, but they are getting steadily better at it.

When changes are made, they most likely are sustaining. And good companies are great at sustaining themselves. Kraft Foods, for example, had a great run in the 1980s and 1990s making infinite variations on their products, with different flavors, packaging, convenience sizes, and so on (eighteen varieties of Chips Ahoy cookies, thirty-one kinds of Oreos, eighteen variations on Philadelphia Cream Cheese, twenty-seven varieties of Balance Bars, and so on). Those are the kinds of changes that big companies are excellent at doing. In these situations, it is easy to retreat from mistakes, because they are made one step at a time.

But the realization that disruption is inevitable is not universal. The recorded music industry has been especially slow to adapt to disruptive change, holding on for dear life to a business model that has been outflanked by circumstance. As the market has shifted with joy to digital music, the recording industry has been dragged along with the greatest reluctance.

BUYING INNOVATION

To head off market disruption, then, most current oligopolies buy serious innovation from the source, mostly in small companies. The likeliest exit for an innovator is to make a splash, and then get bought out by one of the big boys. This method gives the buying company the option of releasing the disruptive product (and getting an edge on other members of the oligopoly). On occasion, it stifles the product by sitting on the patents for its own long-term good. That's what seems to have happened with General Motors' flirtation with the electric-powered car in the late 1990s and early 2000s. Take, for example, the way in which Microsoft and its cohorts have stifled innovation in the computer industry. Or take the way in which the phone oligopoly held up the adoption of DSL high-speed Internet access until they were forced to really make it work, thanks to competition from cable TV companies. By co-opting the disruptions, big companies buy time.

This why PepsiCo and Coca-Cola have invested in bottled water and juices, why Budweiser has bought microbreweries, and why Kraft and General Mills have bought out organic food companies. It explains the purchase of start-up drug companies and biotech firms by Big Pharma. It's why big oil companies invest in solar and wind power, big auto companies keep their hand in electric and hydrogen engine technologies, and why Microsoft went from scoffing at such developments as point-and-click computing and the Internet to dominating them.

Why Innovators Sell Out

Since the profitability of a PowerBar (or any successful innovation) is so much greater than the average on the products from the giant who competes in the same product segment, the giant has to attack the innovator's market share.

That profitability can be high because when a product concept is new, buyers don't have clear value estimates, and (to some extent) price is not as important as it is with a commodity item.

In the long run, the innovator is too small to fight back. With a retail product, it cannot do all the bundling tricks, it cannot threaten to withdraw products from retailers. It cannot distribute into all the nooks and crannies efficiently. It cannot set up regional production facilities. It cannot buy advertising at competitive rates. Most important, it can't easily gain leverage, or even a hearing, with some retailers.

If the innovator doesn't sell out, it will see its profitability diminish over time toward the average. That decline in profits happens first because the innovative product is not as new any more, and second because imitators enter the market. At that point, the product won't be worth as much as it is when its profitability is still high (so, sell now).

The old business model was designed to create a new product and to reinvest the profits into building an empire. For more and more entrepreneurs, the idea is to create a product, make a noise with the brand, and sell out to a large multinational.

Cashing Out Versus Building a New Empire

There are two basic ways to approach building a new company in a competitive field. First, there is the drive to build a long-term independent company. This means having the potential to grow a lasting company, perhaps build a major player, even become a dominant world-class company. Many of the most celebrated names in the business world are companies that started in the last few decades and have gone from nowhere to everywhere. That's the shining example that companies like Amazon, Starbucks, or Nokia represent. And for a significant number of new start-ups, the idea of becoming one of these world-beating companies is a major motivator.

But increasingly, many people start up a company with a more modest goal. They want to build a company to a size and success that can attract outside buyers, a move that is now termed *flipping a start-up*. The period needed to build to that level may be two years or twenty, but the eventual idea is to earn a big payday for the principals and the early investors. In fact, most investment funds that offer seed money are counting on nothing less (and nothing more). The task of sustaining a product or service is to be left to others.

Yet a third group of entrepreneurs starts with the first approach, then switches to the second. The climb from a simple idea to a $1 million or $10 million company is exhilarating. But once you have arrived at a certain amount of success (depending on the business), you become a target for bigger enterprises. Realism sets in, and the founder's main thought is to get out while the getting's good. In general, big companies can make an offer the original principals and investors cannot refuse.

In the food industry, for example, we see a constant parade of companies who end up selling out not long after their brilliant new product concept is proven.

For some companies, this sellout comes after a few years, for others after a few decades. But once they prove their concept, it's likely that a big rival will come knocking on the door. When the choice comes between taking the business to the next level or cashing in on its success, it is likely that the sellout offer will be too good to pass up. After years of scrimping, hard work, and anxiety about making payroll, it's hard to refuse a sum that can make you and your family comfortable for the rest of your lives. The buyer may ask the innovator to stay on in some function, but most acquirees are out the door, one way or another, pretty quickly.

It's noteworthy that many of these companies have the same narrative, including some or all of the phrases "two friends," "health nut," "own kitchen," "a few thousand dollars," "struggled," and so on.

A few notes are necessary to explain Table 4.1. In Snapple's case, the founders sold out to an investment firm and the company was taken public and then quickly bought out by Quaker Foods. Quaker paid $1.7 billion for the company, ran it to the ground, and sold it to a company called Triac for $300 million. Triac eventually sold it to Cadbury Schweppes (for $910 million).

Table 4.1 Food and Beverage Entrepreneurs and Their Buyouts

Product	Innovation	Founded	Bought By	Year
Smartfood	High-end cheese popcorn	1982	Frito-Lay (PepsiCo)	1989
Snapple	Bottled iced tea	1972	Quaker Oats (eventually to Cadbury Schweppes)	1994
Balance Bar	Nutrition bar	1992	Kraft Foods	2000
Ben & Jerry's	Premium ice cream	1970	Unilever	2000
Boca Foods	Soy "hamburger" (Bocaburger)	1993	Kraft Foods	2000
Odwalla	Fresh bottled juice	1980	Coca-Cola	2001
SoBe Beverages	Energy drinks	1996	PepsiCo	2001
Nantucket Nectars	Fresh bottled juice	1990	Cadbury Schweppes	2002
White Wave	Soy milk	1977	Dean Foods	2002
Horizon Organic	Organic milk	1992	Dean Foods	2003
Stonyfield Farms	Organic Yogurt	1983	Danone	2003
Good Earth	Herbal, fruit, and medicinal teas	1972	Tata Tea (India, owner of Tetley)	2005
Scharffen Berger	Premium chocolates	1996	Hershey	2005
IZZE	Sparkling fruit juice	2002	PepsiCo	2006
Stacy's Pita Chips	Flavored pita chips	1997	Frito-Lay (PepsiCo)	2006
Dagoba	Organic chocolates	2001	Hershey	2006

Flipping Out

Especially in technology and biotechnology, many companies are started with the express purpose of being bought out. In the high-tech field, everyone knows that is the game. In fact, it's the avowed purpose of the venture capitalists that fund small start-up tech firms. The dot-com boom of the late 1990s was filled with firms that clearly existed only for the purpose of flipping, as they hadn't the slightest chance of making a go of it as an independent company.

Flipping, at least in the technology industry, is still alive and well, and the term build-to-flip has become common among entrepreneurs. Take, for example, the company Oddpost, which developed a superior, faster e-mail engine. The story involves two friends (unemployed programmers) who started working together in 2002, set up a company in 2003, and after a later investment of $2 million, sold the company (to Internet company Yahoo) for $28 million.

This is a growing phenomenon, according to one expert:

> Oddpost is part of an emerging breed of here-today, bought-tomorrow start-ups that are sprouting with minimal funding, flowering briefly, and being gobbled up by far bigger companies. In many instances, these built-to-flip outfits forego—or sometimes can't get—money from venture capitalists. They instead create shoestring operations focused on the rapid development of narrow technologies to plug gaps in existing product lines or add useful features to existing products. Then they look to a deep-pocketed patron to scoop them up.[16]

That opinion is seconded by another observer of the venture capital scene, who notes the proliferation of companies that exist almost solely to be snapped up. "These folks are unabashed about their intention to be acquired and they are developing their software and services with an eye towards compatibility with their would-be acquirers."[17]

The names of the entrepreneurial companies like Oddpost are known only to a few specialists, but the buyers are often the same caliber of big, multinational players. The transactions outlined in Table 4.2 are from 2005, and the big buyers mentioned also acquired many other small firms, with deals ranging from tens of millions to hundreds of millions of dollars. In each case, the acquirer was looking for some key element or patent that they needed to complement their flagship products.

The list in Table 4.2 is just the tip of the iceberg for one year. As you can see, there's a wide variety of products, and it's not clear what any of them does. These acquisitions were generally not the over-the-top acquisitions of the dot-com boom, but these small companies (some with only two or three employees) all did quite well. Each provided just a little piece of technology that the bigger companies were looking for (pieces that the rest of us may find hard to fathom).

And of course, there is YouTube. In 2006, Google acquired the online video site and its technology with its remarkable interface for $1.65 billion in stock. YouTube was founded in 2005. One day it hardly existed; the next, it was

Table 4.2 A Sample of 2005 Acquisitions of Innovative Tech Start-Ups

Company	Innovation	Founded	Bought By	Year
BindView	Security policy enforcement software	1990	Symantec	2005
del.icio.us	Social bookmarking Web service	2003	Yahoo!	2005
Dodgeball	Social networking by cellphone	2002	Google	2005
IMLogic	Instant messaging security software	2001	Symantec	2005
Innobase Oy	Open-source database software	1995	Oracle	2005
Lighthammer	Manufacturing intelligence software	1998	SAP	2005
Netsift	Network security	2004	Cisco	2005
Niku	IT governance software	1998	Computer Associates	2005
Oblix	Identity management	1996	Oracle	2005
ProClarity	Business analysis tools	1995	Microsoft	2005
Sarvega	XML and self-aware document software	2000	Intel	2005
Sybari Software	Antivirus software	1995	Microsoft	2005
Tarantella (formerly part of SCO)	Server-based application access software	2001 (origins go back to 1979)	Sun Microsystems	2005
Topspin Communications	Programmable network switches	2000	Cisco	2005

everywhere, going from 5 million to 30 unique million viewers a day in six months in 2006. Google had tried to set up a video repository, but YouTube's software made short videos a staple product on the Web.

Curiously enough, every indication is that the two founders weren't even thinking about making big money from the software and the company, and even in May 2006, they were quoted as saying that they weren't interested in selling out or monetizing the product.[18] It's clear that a billion and a half can be very persuasive.

HEDGING BETS: ORGANIC FOOD

Large companies often buy out smaller rivals not only to get their hands on the innovative products or their patents, but also to make sure that they are not unprepared for upcoming trends.

The most dynamic segment of the food business, as we have seen from Table 4.1, is in the growth of organic food. This is a particularly sensitive area for big companies to get into, in that many organic food buyers are actually making as much a political statement as a nutritional one. Many organic food customers resent mass processing of food and oppose companies peddling high-fructose corn syrup like drug dealers handing out heroin samples to an all-to-eager public. Yet many smart organic food lovers are shocked to find out that their favorite food is made by the same people who bring them Velveeta or Froot Loops.

As one source puts it, "We tend to make an implicit assumption that organic food producers are still small farmers who combine ecologically sound farming practices with a political agenda to promote and develop food systems which are local, sustainable, and able to survive independent of corporate agribusiness."[19] That assumption is not very tenable.

For the market-dominating food companies, going organic is a defensive move. A *Fortune* magazine article lays out some of the deals that big food has made to make sure that they won't be in a position of weakness should the green or natural products sector suddenly become far more popular.[20] In fact, the market for organic food has increased by 20 percent a year over the last decade, even though consumers pay a premium price for such products. That's still only about 2 percent of the national food budget, but with many other sectors of that market static, it represents a real growth opportunity. The organic market is likely to grow even further, particularly with the announcement of a serious commitment to organic food on the part of #1 food retailer Wal-Mart (more below).

In 2003, 40 percent of organic food was sold through normal food channels, like Safeway and Kroger. It makes sense that the companies that already have a major presence in those stores would be in a position to sell their organic products first. They are also interested in making sure that new upstarts don't start taking away some of their shelf space.

Here are some of the transactions listed in the article plus a few more:

- In 2004, Danone, the French yogurt and water giant, bought a majority share of Stonyfield Farm. Stonyfield sells organic yogurt products, including drinkable yogurt. Stonyfield products leverage Danone's considerable distribution and manufacturing resources.
- Small Planet Foods was bought by General Mills in 1999. The company sells the brands Muir Glen (canned tomatoes, pasta, salsa) and Cascadian Farms (cereals, frozen foods, pickles, fruit spreads, juice concentrates).
- Kellogg's owns Morningstar Farms (meat substitutes and prepared foods), Worthington Foods (meat substitutes), Natural Choice (meat substitutes, condiments, prepared meals), Loma Linda (organic meat products), and Kashi (whole grain cereals).
- Kraft Foods (Altria) owns Boca (meat substitutes) and Back to Nature.
- Dean Foods, the world's #1 milk company, also owns WhiteWave Foods (tofu and Silk soy milk), Horizon organic milk, and Alta Dena.

- Coca-Cola owns Odwalla organic juices.
- M&M Mars owns Seeds of Change snack foods.
- ConAgra, a leading corn and soybean processor, owns Light Life (meat substitutes).
- Hain Celestial Group is the largest independent organic food processor, with such brands as Celestial Seasonings (tea), Terra Chips, Hain (snacks), Soy Dream, WestSoy (soy milk), Rice Dream (rice milk), Spectrum (dressings), Arrowhead Mills (organic baking supplies), and many more. The company works closely with Heinz, which helps distribute its foods and owns a 20 percent interest.

Expect more mergers and takeovers. The big food companies certainly didn't develop the organic food market, but they are glad to step in now that it is somewhat established and take it over. More than anything, oligopolies fear market disruption from outsiders. The healthy food movement may be just a fad, but Kraft and Kellogg's can't take a chance. They also have the marketing machines to significantly expand demand once they are in the category.

Wal-Mart Goes Organic

In mid-2005, Wal-Mart announced that it would become a major retailer of organic food. According to a *New York Times* story, Wal-Mart is trying to brush up its image to appeal to "urban and other upscale consumers."[21] By entering that market, Wal-Mart, the #1 supermarket company, will instantly become the #1 organic food buyer and reseller. It will also change the concept of organic from elitist to everyday.

Wal-Mart's move will make for a boom in the organics industry and will introduce organic foods to many shoppers who have never been to Whole Foods Market or a health food store. That sounds like a good idea.

But it's not the local farmer or the small, idealistic food packager who are likely to be the beneficiaries of Wal-Mart. It's the big food producers like Kraft and Kellogg's that already supply much of the regular junk food sold by Wal-Mart. After all, this is another case of the big serving the big: only a megacorporation can deliver massive quantities at low prices to Wal-Mart distribution centers.

In addition, the whole concept of organic is likely to be bent and extended (the *Times* article cites organic Rice Krispies and organic macaroni and cheese among other products). Such groceries will use some technically organic elements, but the substitution of organic cane sugar for regular old sugar is unlikely to make them more healthy. Kellogg's, for example, is going to sell organic Frosted Mini-Wheats. As one expert quoted in the *Times* article is quoted as saying, "It's a ploy to be able to charge more for junk food."[22]

MERGER AND ACQUISITION SCLEROSIS

Even when they buy innovation, the need to control can either slow big companies down or make them irrelevant. Mergers and acquisitions (M&As)

can actually make companies less innovative, whatever the intention of the buyout.

As one set of researchers that tried to analyze the relationship between M&A and R&D notes, the innovation declines especially when two companies in direct competition ("substitutive technologies") join up. "We find that when merged firms are technologically substitutive, key employees tend to leave more often, the R&D portfolio becomes more focused, the R&D horizon becomes shorter, and internal funds available to R&D decrease."[23]

Peter J. Solomon, a leading U.S. investment banker, has some experience-based notions about the problems that mergers can run into.[24] According to Solomon,

> The downside of getting bigger is becoming more bureaucratic. It takes a great management team to prevent this. Many mergers fail because it takes a lot of work to merge cultures successfully. People run out of energy, systems, information, or talent. When you reach a certain size, you can outgrow your ability to be innovative. But at that point you can rely on market force. And force can overcome innovation for a hell of a long time.[25]

Solomon makes several points that apply to the new oligopoly. It's a constant struggle for big companies to keep focused and they can be punished severely for biting off more than they can chew. That makes it more imperative than ever to form intelligent, coherent oligopolies, rather than ill-assorted conglomerates.

But, as Solomon says, the sheer inertia of a business juggernaut can make up for a lot of other faults. The bigger the company, the less fatal the mistakes. Only the most egregious errors can hurt your competitive position in the two- or three-tiered company oligopoly. True, your position can be slowly undermined and just occasionally a new trend can disrupt the market. Basically, the companies that have managed to get into a tight oligopoly are able to adapt through brute force, either buying off new competitors or setting up subsidiaries to compete with them.

Only when the whole market is radically changed, as is happening now in the record industry, do these companies suffer badly. (They can suffer when there are too many competitors, when a balanced oligopoly has not yet been established, such as was the case in the cell phone industry and where there is too much real competition.) The company may not match analyst or stockholder expectations, but even that can be addressed through the crude management expedients of downsizing and dropping unprofitable products.

INTELLECTUAL PROPERTY AND OLIGOPOLIES

One strategy that market-dominating companies use to avoid the disruption is the mastery of intellectual property (IP) law. Over the past few decades, the rights of copyright holders and especially patent holders have expanded dramatically, and there's no doubt about who owns most of those copyrights and patents.

The concentration of many industries in the last decade has been accompanied by a spike in IP activity. This has been expressed in terms of a ramp up in lawsuits over copyrights, trademarks, and especially patents. One study by Boston University law professors asserts that "the number of patent lawsuits filed in the United States doubled in the 1990s and evidence is that such lawsuits have kept increasing since."[26] And the number of patents has grown similarly. In 2005, for example, there were a record number of patents applied for, reportedly 8.1 percent higher than 2004. At the same time, the U.S. Patent Office is so choked with patents that it issued fewer in 2005 than in 2004, while the average approval time has extended to almost thirty months.[27]

Most would agree that prudence dictates a reasonable defense of IP. But the defense can quickly go from defense to offense. For the biggest companies, protecting IP often functions as a way to take advantage of their bigness in order to minimize the impact of innovations of small competitors. We might call it "disrupting the disrupters." The ways in which big companies execute the full-court press on patents, copyrights, and trademarks are manifold. This protectiveness is justified by the big company in a number of ways, but a major reason, often unspoken, is to hold the line against such disruptive innovation.

Lawyering Up

One of the advantages that large companies have in the struggle against disruptive ideas is the money to hire a deep legal staff, both internally and externally. Market-dominating companies can marshal a phalanx of lawyers to intimidate smaller competitors. Whether the big company is infringing on ideas for which the smaller one has a patent or whether it is accusing the small one of infringing on its patents, the threat of comparatively bottomless access to the sharpest lawyers is often enough to make the smaller company back off.

As one writer put it, "Patents today are increasingly used to harass, invade and often, as in the highly litigious medical devices industry, eliminate the competition."[28] Big companies collect patents, useful or not, ready to pounce on smaller companies. They know that they can disrupt the operations of a small company simply by forcing them to bulk up their legal staffs. Litigation can take years and chew up millions of dollars, discourage investors, and distract the energies of company executives. Often it seems cheaper just to settle. The problem is that it might make you an inviting target for others. There can always be another knock on the door and a brand-new lawsuit. According to the American Intellectual Property Law Association, the typical patent case can cost $500,000 to $2.5 million, just for legal fees, and can eat up months.[29] That's not counting any penalties for infringement if you lose the case, which can cost up to $100 million or higher. Many small companies prefer to pay a few hundred thousand dollars for a licensing fee.

The issue is significant enough to bother even fairly large companies, like French telephone equipment manufacturer Alcatel, which came clear on this problem in its 2001 annual report:

> Third parties have asserted, and in the future may assert, claims against us alleging that we infringe their IP rights. Defending these claims may be expensive and divert the efforts of our management and technical personnel. If we do not succeed in defending these claims, we could be required to expend significant resources to develop non-infringing technology or to obtain licenses to the technology that is the subject of the litigation.[30]

Patents Run Amok

Patents, originally intended to protect inventors of physical devices, have now been extended to areas like software, surgical procedures, the human genome, seeds, and, worst of all in the United States, the so-called business processes. An overworked patent office is busy accepting patents in areas in which they have little expertise and which they can't see or touch.

In technology, especially, the tendency is to patent everything and leave it up to the courts to sort it all out. In an incisive paper "A New Paradigm for Intellectual Property Rights of Software," attorney Mark H. Webbink notes that breakthrough, multibillion dollar drugs like Pfizer's Viagra and Merck's Zocor are each protected by a single patent. "By comparison, Microsoft has 14 separate patents on the positioning and movement of a cursor, and they have two additional applications pending on it."[31] Companies are no longer using patents to protect significant advances, but rather to create an environment in which "information is being sliced and diced to the point that every trivial combination or extension of prior software technology is being accorded the same protection as a groundbreaking drug."[32]

The idea is that patents are being used not to reward real innovators but to trip them up. As Webbink puts it, "Microsoft is a prime example of patents significantly trailing, rather than leading, innovation and fiscal success, patents having played no meaningful role in the first 10 years of Microsoft's life as a public corporation."[33] Most of Microsoft's patents act as a barrier to entry for small companies.

Copyrights

Although patents are the most obvious way in which big companies use IP laws to stifle competition, there are copyrights as well. A recent *New York Times Magazine* article, "The Tyranny of Copyright," explores the way in which big companies use copyright laws as a weapon to control mind space on the market and threaten competition, criticism, or even reportage.[34] In the last decades, particularly in the United States, oligopolies have successfully extended the tenure and scope of copyrights. What was once a means to protect the rights of writers and musicians for a limited time has now become *the* means for multinational companies to guarantee themselves effortless long-term profits.

The history of copyright law in the United States, as noted by the article, is instructive:

> In 1790, copyright protection lasted for 14 years and could be renewed just once before the work entered the public domain. Between 1821 and 1909, the maximum term was increased from 28 to 53 years. Today, copyright protection for individuals lasts for 70 years after the death of individuals; for corporations, it's 90 years.[35]

That extension has been pushed by those with the most to gain, the biggest media companies. The result has been almost no new work entering the public domain over the past few decades. Even worse has been the mad scramble by entities like music companies, photo archives, and book publishers to snatch up the rights to anything they can get their hands on.

One of the recurrent themes of the new oligopoly is the hoarding of intellectual property. In music, copyrights are snatched up by the big music companies. Massive collections of digital photo archives have been collected. More and more creative professionals work under work-for-hire contracts, giving up all rights to their output. And content and brand names are zealously guarded by phalanxes of litigious attorneys.

The law has also extended the scope of copyright protection, creating what critics have called a "paracopyright," which prohibits not only duplicating protected material but in some cases even gaining access to it in the first place.

Media companies are as focused on accumulating IP as they are in originating new material. In fact, they are more focused, since reselling already successful works requires little overhead and less risk. For example, some of the biggest deals between music companies have had less to do with acquiring current artists (for these may flop or defect to other companies) and more to do with acquiring the backlist of evergreen recordings and song copyrights. These are perennial sources of income, no matter how incompetent the current staff may be at finding new hits.

In addition, the United States is pressuring other countries to match its draconian copyright laws, not just to curb piracy (a legitimate aim) but also to extend the control of the multinational media companies. All this might be fine if it enriched and inspired artists and writers to create better work. Instead, it puts a premium on blockbusters and instant success, distorting any real creativity. In the end, it enriches only a handful of artists, many of whom eventually have to sign away the rights to their own work, just in order to get published or produced.

The ideal situation, which we may be approaching in our digital age, is something called a "permission culture." As the *Times* article explains,

> Whereas you used to own the CD or book you purchased, in the permission culture it's more likely that you will lease (or license) a song, video, or e-book, and even then only under restrictive conditions: read your e-book, but don't copy or

paste any selections; listen to music on your MP3 player, but don't copy and burn it on a CD or transfer it to your stereo.[36]

With the possibility of even further expansion of copyright law, there's a compelling reason for the big media companies to keep buying each other, even if the immediate financial return isn't there. The ownership of copyrights, along with control of the shelf space, actual and virtual, is giving a handful of companies the unbounded power of intellectual property.

This book is not the place to get intro a lengthy discussion of the extension of IP rights and they way in which they have blossomed into a specialist business. And the companies involved will claim that, for them, the best defense against the depredations of others is an aggressive offense. Nevertheless, it is clear that patents are being used much differently than they were even twenty years ago, and the biggest companies, as usual, are getting the biggest benefit from this shift in use.

TO SUM UP

Oligopolies and oligopsonies are not static. They are subject to disruptions, especially from innovations in the market that are out of their control. That has been the death of a number of complacent companies. This is especially a problem because large companies are often weak at developing disruptive innovations internally. The culture of market-dominating companies makes real innovation very difficult.

But modern management is aware of that problem—they take steps to avoid disruption. They buy innovation wherever they see it threatening their position in the market, cutting off the innovators before they become rivals. For small innovative companies, with the need to pay off impatient investors and the difficulties of going from a start-up to a big company, a generous offer is hard to refuse, especially when faced with potential competition in their once-over-looked niche.

One other major technique for large companies is preemptive intellectual property claims, where an aggressively increased and defended set of patents along with extended copyrights is used to keep legal pressure on newer competitors. It's particularly effective on small companies that can afford neither the crack legal staff nor the distraction from everyday business.

In these ways, market dominators try to ward off innovation's threat to their position. Such tactics can never entirely stifle market disruption, but they can and do weaken and postpone it.

5 / Prices and Costs

IF THE CLASSIC THEORY IS CORRECT, the existence of so many oligopolies in the economy should lead to ever higher prices. The point of oligopolies is, by standard reckoning, to allow companies to increase prices. It seems only reasonable to suppose that Big Oil jacks up gas and heating oil prices, Big Agribusiness uses its oligopolies to jack up food prices, and Big Pharma uses it market domination to run up drug prices.

Paradoxically, that is not quite what is happening in the real world, at least not in any pervasive way. In many categories, prices from 1990 to 2006 have stayed remarkably stable, with price rises in most areas reaching a little above the general (and remarkably low) rate of inflation.[1] That's in spite of increasing concentration in almost every sector of the economy.

In some segments, in fact, prices have lagged behind inflation. For example, the cost of flying from New York to Los Angeles is, by inflation-adjusted measure, less expensive in 2007 than it was in 1990. That's in spite of major rises in the cost of airplane fuel. The cost of long-distance telephone service is considerably lower. The price of computers, televisions, and a range of other electronic equipment is lower, even as quality and features have gone up. The cost of clothing, at least at the general consumer level, has been remarkably steady. (That's not to deny that what inflation has occurred hasn't hurt those on fixed incomes or in dead-end jobs, but it's hurt them less than it could have if really unchecked.)

WHAT ABOUT THE VILLAINS?

While many might not believe it, one major factor in moderating the cost of living has been Wal-Mart.[2] That company by itself has put enormous pressures on prices. In fact, a 2005 study by consulting firm Global Insight called "The Economic Impact of Wal-Mart" found that "the expansion of Wal-Mart over the 1985–2004 period can be associated with a cumulative reduction by 9.1 percent in the growth of food-at-home prices, a 4.2 percent reduction in the growth of commodities (goods) prices, and a 3.1 percent reduction in the growth of overall consumer prices as measured by the Consumer Price Index."[3] Of course, the Consumer Price Index has gone up, but, according to the report, it would have gone up by these percentages or more without Wal-Mart. And Wal-Mart competitors in many sectors of retailing (Target, Best Buy, Safeway) have followed suit in holding down prices.

Increases in the price of energy, health care, and real estate have been the biggest causes in the overall cost of living. Many impassioned politicians and editorialists conclude that the dramatic rise in petroleum-based products is the result of a conspiracy among members of the oil oligopoly, those evil-sounding mixes of familiar names: ExxonMobil, ConocoPhilips, and Chevron (which recently changed its name from ChevronTexaco), all of which merged and grew bigger in the 1990s.

While doubtless these companies have learned to take advantage of shortages to skim a few more pennies out of every gallon they refine and sell, the fundamental price has more to do with political and economical conditions far out of the control of "Big Oil." Given stepped-up nationalization of oil assets in countries like Venezuela and Russia, political problems in places like Iraq and Nigeria, the unabashed (if hard-to-manage) OPEC cartel, and the increasing demands of the growing Chinese market, the real price rises of a barrel of oil are only marginally affected by the U.S. oil oligopoly. In fact, oil prices, though fluctuating, stayed at levels close to $25 a barrel (in current dollars) through the 1990s. Big Oil executives weren't keeping the price low out of the goodness of their hearts back then, and they haven't really been behind the doubling of prices we've seen in recent years.[4]

Real estate is another area in which there have been major price rises over the past fifteen years.[5] That's another area that can't be explained by a conspiracy of evil property owners and wealthy real estate investors. Residential real estate is among the most unconcentrated markets out there, and any idea that Century21, RE/MAX, and Prudential are conspiring to raise prices of local housing is belied by the fact that those companies have tighter profit margins than ever, caused by declining commissions (probably thanks to the competition from the Internet).[6] If it's a conspiracy, it's one willingly participated in by all homeowners.

Health care is yet another matter, and there's good evidence that the lessening competition between insurers and the power of the pharmaceutical companies have contributed to higher prices. In 2005, for example, health care costs rose by 7.9 percent, three times higher than the rate of overall inflation.[7] We'll discuss the pharmaceutical industry more extensively in Chapter 8, but health care is the one sector where business concentration seems to be, at least in some ways, related to increased prices.

One other area where prices have risen well above the general rate of inflation is in the area of luxury goods. Prices of such items as art, fine jewelry, luxury automobiles, Italian leather goods, and fine wines are going up much faster than the prices at Wal-Mart or Target. As one journalist notes, "*Forbes*' Cost of Living Extremely Well Index, which tallies the rise in costs of items such as Gucci loafers, Harvard tuition, caviar, and Steinway pianos, has been rising far more rapidly than the consumer price index in recent years."[8] Part of this is due to a weaker dollar in the past decade—raising the prices Americans pay for Porsches and fine Bordeaux; part is due to the increasing number of rich people competing for a limited supply of some goods—such as Sevruga caviar or Picasso drawings. Resistance against higher prices for high-status goods is lessening as the rich get a lot richer, thanks to U.S. tax policies. Again, there is no conspiracy of oligopolies, since, in most cases, it is scarcity that adds value in this area.

Evidence of massive across-the-board price rises thanks to the general concentration of industry is just not there. Prices do go up, and in some areas they go up considerably, but only occasionally is that because of a conspiracy.

COLLUSION AND CARTELS

But collusion does happen, and it's not a relic from the days of Rockefeller and the robber barons. Settled oligopolies should not have to act as cartels, fixing prices by meeting in secret.

Cartels, out-and-out price-fixing conspiracies, still happen in a variety of industries. The temptation is always there to fix prices, and it's easy to conspire. We know it happens because some companies get caught and fined, and we can assume some others don't get caught. The companies generally admit nothing, but often pay the fine. And those that are caught are probably just the tip of the iceberg, the ones that are foolish enough to be easily detected and who allow a case to be built against them.

Here are some examples of recently busted cartels:

- In 2002, the big five recording companies and three of the biggest music retailers were found to be fixing CD prices. The industry was charged with keeping CD prices artificially high in the 1990s with a policy called "minimum advertised-pricing." The arrangement was that the recording companies paid for retailers' ads, in return, the stores agreed to sell CDs at above retail prices. The lawsuit, led by state governments, ended in major fines. The record company participants were Universal Music, Sony Music, Warner Music, BMG Music, and EMI Group, and the retailers were Musicland Stores, Trans World Entertainment, and Tower Records.[9]
- In 2002, the British Department of Health sued a cartel of six generic drugmakers for fixing prices on two of the most frequently prescribed drugs, namely the blood-thinning drug Warfarin and various penicillin drugs. Both are generic drugs that were marked up 400 percent or more over their precartel prices.[10]
- Auction houses Sotheby's and its rival Christie's were caught fixing fees and commissions for their services. The two dominate the field, with

no third company even close. In 2001, Sotheby's ex-chairman Alfred Taubman was found guilty of conspiring with Christie's ex-chairman Anthony Tennant to fix prices for their services. Taubman was sentenced to a year in prison and was fined $7.5 million. The two companies agreed to pay $20 million to settle a class-action settlement with some customers.[11]

- In 2000, three European and three Japanese companies, who together controlled more than 80 percent of the world's vitamin market, agreed to settle charges that they had conspired to fix prices for vitamins and vitamin products. The suit brought by New York state and others was settled for $225 million. Then–New York Attorney-General Eliot Spitzer explained, "The companies met in secret, in locations around the world, to carry out illegal agreements that imposed a hidden 'vitamin tax' on shoppers that drove up weekly grocery bills and cost consumers and businesses hundreds of millions of dollars over the past decade."[12] The six vitamin companies are Swiss-based Hoffman-La Roche Inc., Germany-based BASF Corp., French-based Aventis Animal Nutrition S.A. (formerly Rhone-Poulenc Animal Nutrition), and three Japanese companies—Takeda Chemical Industries Ltd., Eisai Co. Ltd, and Daiichi Pharmaceutical Co. Ltd.

- In 2002, the European Union (EU) fined five companies for operating a citric acid cartel. The commission imposed fines of 135 million euros on U.S.-based Archer Daniels Midland (ADM), Swiss Jungbunzlauer AG, Hoffmann-La Roche, Germany's Bayer AG, and Cerestar Bioproducts, a French company now owned by U.S. agribusiness giant Cargill. ADM already had lost a similar suit in 1998 in the United States. Citric acid is used widely in the food and beverage processing, cosmetics, and chemical industries.[13]

And the list goes on. Both U.S. and EU antitrust regulators are aggressive in prosecuting cartels when they find them. As Joel Klein, in charge of the Clinton administration's Department of Justice antitrust effort, said, "International cartels typically pose an even greater threat to American businesses and consumers than do domestic conspiracies, because they tend to be highly sophisticated and extremely broad in their impact—both in terms of geographic scope and in the amount of commerce affected by the conspiracy."[14]

As markets become increasingly international, so can price-fixing conspiracies cross national borders and threaten to fall between jurisdictions. When cartels are formed, they are increasingly global in nature.

SIGNALING AND OLIGOPOLIES

Price-fixing, then, is often detected and punished—engaging in a conspiracy can be very risky. Conversely, a long-term price war is dangerous for all competitors in any industry, where all the participants can get burned badly. However, there is a third way, usually legal, that oligopolies use to stabilize price. That alternative is price signaling.

Signaling is a way for members of an oligopoly to coordinate prices without having to actually talk to each other about it. It's all about setting points of equilibrium in a market by setting your own prices in keeping with those of others. In a tight oligopoly, there is less likely to be a rogue seller who will not participate in the "gentlemen's agreement" to maintain steady price ranges.

Signaling is a favorite subject of role-playing experiments in college economics classes, and based on game theory, mutual cooperation is the best solution for all the participants. But trusting other participants is never easy.

Such trust can only be built by playing the game continually and closely watching the behavior of the other participants. Coke and Pepsi have played the game for so long that they are comfortable anticipating each other's behavior. Likewise the recording companies have a comfort level that one of them is not going to sell pop music CDs at $5 or $10 less than the competition, except in a short-term sale. The gasoline companies respond quickly to the ups and downs of each other's prices, so there's no point in trying to corner the market by risking margins.

In most oligopolies, signaling prices is often sufficient, and eliminates the need to conspire and leave a paper trail. Antitrust regulators can look critically at obvious signaling, but if the companies keep it discreet, there's not much the watchdogs can do about it legally. So Coke and Pepsi, ExxonMobil and Shell, can generally set prices at levels that match mutual profit requirements, with neither price wars nor secret meetings.[15]

As an article in the journal *Antitrust* notes,

> Firms in an oligopoly may decide to forgo a price cut because they assume their competitor will match the cut, thus providing little long-term benefit. Similarly, a firm in an oligopoly may take a price increase hoping its competitors will follow suit—if they do, a higher equilibrium will prevail; if they do not, the market returns to the status quo ante.[16]

This pattern is called "offer and acceptance."[17] As the article points out, "the price leader makes an 'offer' to its competitors by raising its price, the competitors accept (or not) depending on whether they follow."[18] This is a form of collusion, indeed, but one that leaves no trail of evidence, and one that can be accomplished without any communication between the principals. It's not very far from the course of perfectly honest competition, where a price change by a key competitor forces a response. So that when Samsung starts selling color laser printers for under $500, for example, Hewlett-Packard and Lexmark and the rest are quick to respond with their price cuts or new models that match the new price.

Signaling at Internet Speed

The Internet has made the cycle of signaling even more efficient. Vendors in many industries can see what the competition is doing immediately, just by logging on, and they can react by adjusting their own prices. This is a far cry from the days when price books were set in type and could not be changed for months. Now most prices can be adjusted several times a day, if needed.

That's a game that the airlines are particularly adept at. As consumers have more transparent access to real-time flight pricing through online services like Orbitz and Travelocity, so the airlines are almost obligated to adjust to each other. And on routes where there is no rogue player, like Southwest Airlines or JetBlue, they are (within limits) free to adjust prices upward. As long as the members of the oligopoly with real selling power tacitly agree that a major price war is not in their interest, chances are that prices can quickly readjust themselves, keeping in mind the balance of costs and optimal prices for maintaining profitable sales levels.

The Federal Trade Commission (FTC) and its European equivalent (the European Commission) keep looking closely at e-business signaling, and a variety of opinions are held as to when signaling is a conspiracy or simply the dynamics of the market playing themselves out. One thing is certain, the combination of oligopolies and easy-to-adjust electronic pricing is a recipe for signaling, and it can be done perfectly in the open, without any documented collusion.[19]

Gasoline Signaling

One typical scenario for signaling is in the retail gasoline market, a sore point in recent times. In times when changes in the price and availability of either petroleum or refined gasoline are common, gas stations constantly readjust their prices. Some of that readjustment is based on the actual price they pay refiners for the gasoline. But just as important are the prices of local competitors.

During a general rise in prices, new high prices set by the station down the street "give permission" for the other local stations to follow suit. The price rises faster than is justified by actual costs. On the way down, prices decrease more slowly than the decline in the price of gasoline from the refiners. And it's remarkable how much in step gas stations are on both the up and downside of pricing. As a *BusinessWeek* article puts it, "Why don't gas stations immediately cut their prices when the cost of the fuel they buy goes down? Because they're trying to maximize their profits.... Eventually, though, the fear of losing business forces all stations to cut prices to what the market will bear."[20]

The best part is that no secret meetings or phone calls are needed, not even industrial spying. Everyone's gas prices are posted so conspicuously that you don't even have to slow your car to collect the data. In few other areas are price changes so physically apparent, but for almost all publicly sold goods, pointing and clicking should have the same quick-comparison effect.[21]

WHY ARE PRICES STABLE?

Price hikes have been limited in the past two decades for most companies. Yet many top corporations are showing record profits. If the prices they charge have gone up in a limited way, this growth in net income can only be attributed to reduced costs.

Bringing costs down, rather than pushing prices up, is the secret of Wal-Mart, and, given Wal-Mart's example, it has been the obsession of many companies. Of course, all companies have cut costs to the best of their abilities, but the last twenty years have enabled that approach in a way that has never been seen before. That's primarily due to three factors:

- Global free trade and the lowering of tariffs
- Information technologies that makes coordinating with suppliers easier than ever
- A whole new industry of expediting the delivery of goods worldwide

With these factors, discussed in Barry C. Lynn's book *End of the Line*, global oligopsonies are able to break their ties with local suppliers, or at least threaten to break them. They have changed the whole power balances among companies. "Power over the production system has shifted from the companies that view themselves as manufacturers and producers into the hands of companies designed mainly to trade in the production system, and which never had any reason to identify, track, and limit risk in the production system."[22]

Part of the ability to lower costs comes from such added efficiencies in companies' operations, but a more critical part to lowering costs comes from the power that these companies have over the production system to decrease the costs of the goods and services that the biggest companies buy.

COST-FIXING

As we have shown, market dominators are often oligonomies, both oligopolies and oligopsonies. We call the power of oligopsony to set the prices they will pay for products supplied to them *cost-fixing*. Cost-fixing is the mirror image of price-fixing, just as an oligopsony is a mirror image of an oligopoly. We've discussed this briefly in Chapter 2 in the section titled "Squeezing Suppliers."

Needless to say, the cost fixers vigorously deny any wrongdoing and they have the ability to finance legal appeals, discourage government oversight, and bar any new laws that target their activities. Suppliers who protest against the setup, unless they are unusually well organized and are unique suppliers, can be punished by being bypassed in favor of a more compliant group in another state or country. And most of this manipulation goes on away from any public outrage, particularly when consumer prices are held low.

Like price-fixing, cost-fixing does not require a meeting in a closed room. Competitors know that it's in their mutual interest not to compete too hard on cost *or* price. Once there are only a few buyers, they can signal acceptable costs to each other, just as they signal acceptable prices. Such silent cooperation is almost impossible to regulate or litigate against. It is commonplace, and it is

Globalism and Shifting Costs

In his book *End of the Line*, Barry C. Lynn writes about the vicissitudes of General Motors (GM) in the 1980s and early 1990s, a period when GM was in almost as bad a plight as it is now. At one point, GM brought in Spanish executive Jose Ignacio Lopez from their European operations to run their purchasing operations. Lopez helped revive the company's fortunes at the time by driving ever harder deals with GM's suppliers.

What's interesting to us is that Lopez's actions were part of a bigger movement, namely squeezing the suppliers. As Lynn points out, "Up to 90 percent of the value of any product is created before the final assembly process, and the manufacture of small parts and components is often scattered among hundreds of small plants."[23]

Much of the work at the big auto companies in the 1980s, according to Lynn, was in improving the assembly line. Robotics, ergonomics, and computers were integrated and quality control was improved. Yet that wasn't enough. The real efficiencies were to be gained in the 90 percent of the work that happened before it reached the final plant.

As Lynn points out, the automotive industry had at that point a cozy relationship with its suppliers, who had their little plants clustered around big GM plants and who could expect fair treatment as long as their deliveries were on time and according to specs delivered by GM engineers. GM gave the marching orders and handled all the coordination.

Lopez changed all that. He heaped far more responsibility on the suppliers, centralized more purchasing requirements on fewer firms, and made these bigger supplier firms coordinate the design, manufacturer, and supply chain for subsystems. The end job of the suppliers was to minimize the cost of the components they delivered and to lower the cost of final assembly.

> Lopez was calling on his suppliers not merely to cut their prices but to assume much more of the responsibility for the overall manufacturing process.... This, he believed, would allow a complete redesign of the final assembly system, as suppliers would now be called on to deliver a few very large clusters of components, or subassemblies, to the lead manufacturer, where a greatly stripped-down continent of workers would quickly bolt the pieces together.[24]

Soon enough, the suppliers started moving offshore to meet the demands of the manufacturer. The assembly line was made simpler, requiring fewer workers and minimizing variability. GM became more than ever a marketing and design company, with more and more of the manufacturing outsourced.

The benefit for GM was a cut in costs, both for components and for its own unionized payroll. GM was once the biggest employer in the United States and one of its most generous. By the end of the decade, its workforce shrunk, and its payroll has been surpassed by the much lower-cost payrolls of Manpower and Wal-Mart.

This change, along with the SUV boom, gave GM over a decade of renewed life. More particularly, it serves as a model for other companies, in defense, in electronics, in appliances, in aeronautics, that have followed GM's lead. While the old brand names still remain and some assembly is done in the United States, the big factories are increasingly empty.

most easily seen in the outsourcing of manufacturing work to the developing world.[25] Companies from Nike to Hasbro to Cisco are expert at playing suppliers one against the other, threatening to find other sources, perhaps even in another company, if cost, quality, or delivery goals are not met. The time-tested practice of stretching out payments to suppliers seems to be growing as well.[26] The supplier of an oligopsony has nowhere else to turn.

Far more situations exist, with issues that never get out in the open because the suppliers are too afraid, too disorganized, too poor, or, eventually, are driven out of business. One well-known case is Vlasic Pickles, which got into bed with Wal-Mart, only to have the giant retailer roll over and crush the smaller company. The history of the bankrupting of Vlasic (now owned by Pinnacle Foods) is told at length in various places.[27] One article sums it up well:

> Vlasic Corporation found itself bound to supply huge gallon jars of pickles to Wal-Mart for $2.97, a price at which it made maybe a penny a jar. An "abundance of abundance," the jars' sales went through the roof and became a "devastating success" for Vlasic.... "A family can't eat them fast enough." Forced to continue offering the deal or lose its entire Wal-Mart account, the company saw its profits squeezed for two and a half years before Wal-Mart finally let it "up for air."[28]

As Wal-Mart profiler Charles Fishman observes, "Wal-Mart's focus on pricing, and its ability to hold a supplier's business hostage to its own agenda, distorts markets in ways that consumers don't see, and in ways suppliers can't effectively counter. Wal-Mart is so large that it can often defy the laws of supply, demand, and competition."[29]

Like price-fixing, cost-fixing is sometimes the result of direct collusion (as with tobacco prices). But often it is the result of excess capacity allowing oligopsonies to twist suppliers until they cry "uncle." Wal-Mart needs no collusion with others, since it has such market power on its own and does not need many vendors.

Tyson's Cost-Fixing Lawsuit

Tyson Foods in 2004 lost a federal lawsuit in which it was found that the company had illegally held down the prices it paid to cattle producers. (The lawsuit was filed in 1996, long before Tyson, the leading chicken packer, acquired IBP, the leading beef packer.) The jury fined Tyson Foods $1.28 billion in damages, to be distributed among some 35,000 ranchers. It was thought that it might usher in a new approach to antitrust suits with serious impact on a number of oligopolies, both in the meat industry and outside.

A *Wall Street Journal* article noted that

> the verdict is the biggest yet in a growing area of litigation against a type of antitrust abuse known as monopsony, which is the mirror image of monopoly. While a monopoly usually involves a seller trying to raise the prices paid by consumers,

a monopsony materializes when a firm acquires enough buying power to push down unfairly the prices it pays to its suppliers.[30]

Actually, Tyson is an oligopsony, not a monopsony, because there are at least a few other serious competitors in the cattle-buying industry. The issue here is what we call cost-fixing. The article points out the relationship of this case to the practices of Wal-Mart, and notes that prosecutors have been reluctant to pursue oligopsonists because of the narrow difference between regular price-cutting and illegal anticompetitive activities (cost-fixing).

This suit, which was based on never-used provisions of a 1921 law, had to do with the prevalence of lock-in contracts that forced the price of the few cattle sold on the market lower. In other words, the charge was that the big meat producers had rigged the auction of cattle to the disadvantage of ranchers. Rivals Cargill and Swift also were inspected for similar issues.

The big difficulty was in proving that Tyson deliberately used its market power to fix costs, by taking advantage of the minimal competition and by signaling acceptable biding levels to its rivals. Such cases are always hard to prove, and companies have many ways in which they can adjust the rules of the game to avoid the outright appearance of collusion. And because this has no direct relation to higher consumer prices (indeed, it often leads to steady or somewhat lower consumer prices), government bodies see little urgency in pursuing this matter.

Tyson, which buys around one-third of all cattle sold in the United States, declared that it does not manipulate the market, and that recent rises in beef prices paid to cattlemen is proof of that lack of control. Tyson eventually managed to persuade both a district and an appeals court that the case should be thrown out.[31] The ultimate vindication of Tyson's policies looks like a green light for similar cost manipulation by oligopsonies.

RISK AND OLIGOPOLIES

Another way market dominators lower costs is by shifting risks. Shifting risk is a standard economic activity. We'd all like to hand off the potential downsides of our actions, while keeping the upside. In the business world, it's a way of life and always has been. The new oligopolies have become masters at that game, as risk-shifting has turned into a central and deliberate activity for bigger companies.

Now, offloading risk between equals is a perfectly neutral procedure. Companies offload liability risks to insurance companies, who set their rates to make a profit. Insurance companies in turn sell off some of their risk to reinsurance firms, so that the negative effects of bad luck can be spread out. These deals are essentially even-handed—each side figures out what the risk is worth, and if they can't agree, they go elsewhere. Adam Smith would smile.

But when oligopsonies or oligopsonies exist in relation to a number of small suppliers or buyers, the big firms can forcibly offload risk on those companies that depend on them. It's not as much price-gouging but risk-gouging that gives oligopolies their power in the current market.

Examples of offloading risk include the following:

- Big electronic companies like Dell and Apple, for example, outsource much of the components that make up their machines to third-party companies in China and other Asian countries. When demand goes up, those suppliers are under furious pressure to expand production, never mind the cost, or risk losing part of the contract, possibly all of it. Should demand go down, the suppliers are not compensated for their overcapacity.

- The big meat companies (Tyson, Cargill, Smithfield Foods, and a few others) shift the risk of volatile livestock prices and the unpredictability of weather, feed prices, and disease by shifting risk onto the cattle ranchers, hog farmers, and chicken growers that supply them. Those little guys take the risk, and if they fail, they pay the price. If market prices go up, both the farmers and meatpackers prosper. If prices go down, the farmers bear the load, while the packers continue to collect their markup. Furthermore, the meatpacking companies dictate in almost every way how the farmers work: feed, medical treatment, delivery dates. These farmers are employees of the companies who buy from them in almost every way except in one—they invest their own money into the job, and their paycheck is highly variable. A similar pattern is true with most agricultural commodities. As one writer put it, "agribusinesses that contract with farmers are shifting risks and responsibilities from the company to the farmers. For example, such contracts place all risk and responsibility for environmental harm, quality, production efficiency, disease control, and so forth on the farmer."[32]

- Wal-Mart's suppliers run a sometimes rewarding and sometimes ruinous race. As just-in-time sellers to an enormous and demanding company, they take on heavy-duty, stressful responsibility. They are under obligation to deliver products exactly to Wal-Mart specifications, just in time, and to keep cutting prices. But to meet those demands, the suppliers have to make large investments in plants and operations and have to bite the bullet if, for some reason, the market for their products fizzles or they can't meet all of Wal-Mart's new requirements on price and supply. As Fishman puts it, "Wal-Mart is, in fact, a genius at shifting work, and costs, that have traditionally been handled by retailers back to manufacturers."[33]

- Other retailers have learned their lessons after being "schooled" by Wal-Mart. They avoid risks by changing from the old inventory model where they pay in advance for the goods they sell and swallow the costs if they don't sell. Now, the trend is basically to rent shelf space to other companies, who get paid only when their products go out the door. This has long been the pattern in the book industry, and other industries (most notably supermarkets) are doing it more and more. The retailers end up selling everything on consignment.

- Companies also offload risk to employees. As economist Paul Krugman wrote about Enron, "The case shows how adept corporate executives have become at shifting risk away from themselves and onto others, in particular onto their employees."[34] This means a gradual withering away of benefits, pensions, health insurance, and job security. In his book, *The Great Risk Shift*, Jacob Hacker writes about the demise of traditional notions of the mutual relationship between workers and employers, with the latter now "shifting the major risks of skill obsolescence, unexpected benefit costs, and business fluctuations from corporations onto workers."[35]

Offloading risks in this way is a deliberate, proven route for oligopolies. There was a time when companies tried to build it all themselves, from owning the iron mines and the barges and steel plants, to running the factories and trucks. New oligopolies have found that such extensive vertical integration compounds risks, because all parts of companies suffer when demand goes down for whatever reason. But when big companies can dictate terms to suppliers and to workers, they can let others take the risk while losing little of the reward.

INTRACOMPANY TRADE

One of the least understood activities of large multinational companies is that of intracompany trade. This phenomenon defies some of the rules of supply and demand that have governed the worldwide distribution of cash and labor. When, for example, Apple Computer ships iPods from its plant in China or Xerox imports copiers manufactured mostly in China, it's not obvious when the value is added to trans-shipped goods. That's unlike the classical model of trade where an independent American company, for example, buys French wine or German machine tools at a certain price, then carries them across the ocean to be resold. The relationship between the initial cost of the import and its final price is clear.

Intracompany trade is fuzzy because the deal is often structured as one between a corporation set up in, say, Thailand, and another one in the United States, both subsidiaries of the same parent operation. How much of the difference between the cost of components and raw materials and the final price is assigned to the foreign operation, and how much to the U.S. unit? The "price" that one division pays another is a matter of interpretation. And it's not a trivial matter—if the value is added in the United States, the parent company is liable for U.S. taxes; if the value is added in Thailand, then (lower) Thai taxes apply.

The issue is called *transfer pricing*, an accounting practice whereby "prices for transfers of goods, services, technology, and loans between their worldwide affiliates differ considerably from the prices which unrelated firms would have had to pay."[36] National tax laws and the rulings of the OECD (Organisation for Economic Co-operation and Development) have managed to close some of the biggest loopholes in this area, but such regulations are most useful when it is possible to establish a market value for the goods in question. This isn't easy when we are talking about the internal manufacturing operations of a company with noncommodity products.

One of the most notable transfer pricing lawsuits regulators have prosecuted in the United States is against Swiss watchmaker Swatch in 2004. The company

> funnelled the paperwork for many watches through a subsidiary called Swatch Group (Asia), based in Hong Kong and registered in the tax haven of the British Virgin Islands. SG (Asia) added significant mark-ups to the prices of goods sent to it from other parts of the group before sending them on internally.[37]

Clear? Well, if not, that's what the accountants were aiming for. The matter had not been resolved as this book went to press.

And any multinational can play the game. Cargill, for example, buys soybeans in Brazil and processes them there in at least six plants. If the product is shipped to a Cargill subsidiary in the United States, Europe, or Asia, the exact value of the imported soy products is not easy to determine. Similar problems exist in accounting for auto parts, clothing, beverages, and a range of other products.

Transfer pricing may help answer the question of why the sinking dollar has not helped the U.S. trade balance, as economists generally thought it would. According to a 2005 *Wall Street Journal* story,

> Economic theory says that as the dollar declines, the trade balance should shift in the U.S.'s favor, usually with a delay of about 18 months after the currency starts moving downward. But it has been more than three years since the dollar started its slide, although it has recovered some ground recently, and there is little evidence of a significant impact on trade.[38]

The answer, according to the article, may be that the figures are hopelessly skewed by the moving of goods between foreign and U.S. subsidiaries of large multinationals. In fact, the article states that 42 percent of all U.S. trade in goods in the previous year, $950 billion, came from such intracompany trading.

It's much to the advantage of multinationals to overstate the somewhat arbitrary value of the products they produce in developing countries. That means that the value added in the United State (that which is subject to U.S. taxes) is lower, thus lowering the tax bill. Typically, the tax policies in Malaysia, China, and Brazil will be far less onerous, and a large company providing lots of jobs in the local economy is likely to get a tax break. Large companies have all kinds of leeway in describing the tax venue where they make their biggest profit, because the numbers are even more portable than the goods.

"COST-SIDE" OLIGOPOLIES

In dealing with oligopolies and oligopsonies, classical economics puts a strong emphasis on price competition. A substantial portion of the economics papers on the subject takes oligopoly simply as a way of manipulating prices. But prices in the United States over the last decades, as we have seen, have been relatively stable in spite of greatly increased market concentration.

This realization has modified the antitrust crusade of government antitrust organizations in the United States and the EU. A critical factor in their deliberations is anxiety about inflationary pressures from higher prices. The regulators have seen concentration in every industry with little overall pressure on prices. The growing belief is that oligopolies can be price-neutral. For that reason, many mergers and acquisitions that were turned down in the past are now being allowed, with only minor conditions.

So now we have some economists claiming that oligopolies are in fact beneficial, making more and better products possible at comparable prices thanks to the reeducation of competition. All this is based on what might be termed price-side considerations. Since oligopolies in most areas have not generated the upward pressure that trustbusters might have expected, consumers generally don't care about growing consolidation, as long as they get goods for acceptable prices.

But there is another area in which market-dominating companies work. We can call these cost-based effects. The real reason that oligopolies can hold the line on consumer prices is that they can drive down the costs of doing business. They do this in several ways:

- *Oligopolies increase efficiencies.* The claims of synergy and economies of scale in larger organizations are always exaggerated, but they do exist. In the best sense, large companies have used computers to implement just-in-time strategies that do a better job of ensuring that just enough and not too much of any product or supply is available. Even though increased bureaucracy in larger companies can get in the way, combining administration, buying, and distribution can reduce costs significantly. Likewise, vertical integration (although it's become less common) can take another layer of profit-taking out of the equation.
- *Oligopolies put price pressure on their suppliers.* Wal-Mart, as we have seen, keeps its prices low by offering less to the companies that supply them with the products they sell. In the end, the supplier facing an oligopsony has little choice but to go along. (Suppliers that produce a unique product, say Coca-Cola or Marlboros, have a little more leeway.) But, as we've shown with Wal-Mart and the music industry, only a few products are absolute consumer must-haves.
- *Oligopolies put indirect pressures on the suppliers.* "Slotting fees," the costs that vendors of retail products pay to get on the shelves at Safeway or Home Depot are a good example. This growing practice forces

suppliers to share the cost of getting products on the shelves and marketing them. Such ancillary fees are a growing part of all retailing and many other industries. Suppliers are being asked, as in the book industry, to take all responsibility for unsold inventory, reducing the oligopsony's exposure.

- *Oligopolies put pressure on the wages and benefits of their employees.* That includes taming or busting unions. The lower number of companies in the same field means that even skilled employees have fewer options. And competitors can point to the low wages and benefits of a competitor as arguments for tightening their own employees' belts to survive. That's what's now going on in California, where supermarket chains squeezed unions in 2005 to prepare themselves to compete better with Wal-Mart, which threatened to drive the chains out of business because of lower labor costs.
- *Oligopolies can export jobs to lower-cost labor markets.* Not just manufacturing jobs, although plenty of those are sent overseas, but also more and more white collar jobs, as medical transcriptions move to Pakistan, computer programming moves to India, and customer call centers move to the Philippines. Even the threat of these moves can keep wages and benefits down in the United States.
- *In manufacturing, at least, oligopolies can play one country against another in an attempt to find the lowest-price producer.* So now the relatively "higher" wages of Mexico or Malaysia are making those countries lose jobs to China and Vietnam.

Both direct cost saving and influence-based cost avoidance are arts that only big concentrated companies can perform well. They reduce costs and allow companies to maintain or even reduce prices, while increasing margin. All of these moves can exist without oligopolies and oligopsonies, but oligopolies get a compound benefit, managing to make money and raise barriers for would-be competitors that can't master all these skills quickly.

Another cost-side benefit comes from the manipulation of public policy, whereby big companies arrange matters through legislation and regulation to lower costs and risks. We discuss this subject in the next chapter.

6 / Oligopolies and Public Policy

POSSIBLY THE MOST COMPELLING long-run reason for gaining market share and building an oligopoly is the increased ability to affect, even control, government actions. Given the sophistication of modern lobbying and the cozy relationships that are possible between the regulators and the regulatees, the biggest companies are in a powerful position to influence public policy in their favor.

"Getting the government off our backs" has been a rallying cry for free marketeers and corporate executives, but in reality many companies are eager to keep the government's hand in the market, as long as it favors their interests. So while companies lobby for corporate taxes to be lowered and regulations wiped off the books, they also connive to get interest-free loans, no-bid contracts, trade and tax advantages, along with ever stronger intellectual property laws.

Moreover, since almost every industry is profoundly affected by governmental decisions—about employment laws, safety and environmental regulations, pension liability, health insurance, hiring and firing regulations, antitrust regulation, and many more—all large companies have become more and more overtly eager to bend government policy, locally, nationally, and now internationally. Most companies now work on multiple fronts to further, or at the very least protect, those interests. If they don't, their competitors will gain an advantage over them.

Of course, influencing government decisions is a constant in history—supplying stones for the Pyramids was doubtless a no-bid contract with ample kickbacks and no-show jobs for relatives. The historic record shows no end of favors granted to people or groups close to those in power. But today's megacorporations have become increasingly clever at wielding their power, power that's much more complex to obtain in a fragmented economy. And while companies would have been happy in earlier times to influence the actions of a city or a state, it is now routine to aspire to determine policies both nationally and internationally.

AREAS OF INFLUENCE

The catalog of benefits that governments can confer on corporations is almost endless, but it falls into a number of distinct categories. These benefits don't apply to every industry, but great is the variety of possible returns on the investment of a political contribution, golf trips, speaking fees, consulting contracts for relatives, political action committees, and cash kickbacks. Of course, not all kinds of companies can get these benefits, but the practice has become bigger and more systematic over the part decade.

The key areas in which big companies seek to shape government policy are as follows:

- Obtaining preferential loans, tax breaks, and zoning regulations
- Diminishing the severity of laws regarding pensions, health benefits, working hours, minimum wages, and other employment standards
- Minimizing safety, tax, fraud, and environmental regulation and enforcement
- Weakening the power of labor unions and putting obstacles in the way of organizing labor
- Reducing corporate liability, especially from class-action lawsuits
- Subverting government procurement processes through no-bid contracts and lax auditing and enforcement
- Weakening the enforcement of antitrust laws by the government
- Getting direct subsidies for doing what it might have done in any case, like training workers
- Eliminating restrictions, outsourcing, offshoring, and trade
- Strengthening intellectual property laws to stifle competition and innovation

While not all of these areas apply to all industries, the advantage of pressing on a number of these fronts is becoming more and more apparent to every big company. The catalog of companies, organizations, and trade associations that are now appointing directors and vice presidents of government affairs, once limited to defense firms, now ranges from Monsanto to Harley-Davidson, from Target to Robert Mondavi.

LOBBYING

Is this influence criminal? In some cases, yes. We need look no further than the growing roll of indicted U.S. congressmen and the influence of Jack Abramoff. A lot of noise is made about those who are caught breaking the law, but most influencing of policy is expressed through perfectly legal means. (Of course, those regulations and laws about what lobbyists can and cannot do are written and often enforced by the very people who are being persuaded with gifts, contributions, and sweetheart deals.)

Big corporations don't always get their way. For one thing, there are often competing interests, from other companies, from unions, from voters, and from interest groups whether conservative, liberal, or agnostic. For example, the Big Oil companies, in spite of intense lobbying, have still not managed to open up the Alaska National Wildlife Refuge for drilling, because of countervailing public sentiment. Fear of mad cow disease had served to tighten (just a bit and reluctantly in the United States) cattle feeding standards. Upstart competitors win government contracts, sometimes just by delivering a better proposal. When the media shines a spotlight on some of the most egregious cases of influence peddling and looting of the public treasury, a cry for reform arises and some of the excesses are rolled back, for a while.

But attempts to influence government persist. U.S. companies report spending billions of dollars on lobbying, the most conspicuous form of influencing policy. According to a *Washington Post* story, "The number of registered lobbyists in Washington has more than doubled since 2000 to more than 34,750 while the amount that lobbyists charge their new clients has increased by as much as 100 percent."[1] (Other industries should grow half so fast!) Furthermore, a *San Jose Mercury News* story reports one lobbying concern, "The Carmen Group, a mid-size firm, has calculated that for every $1 million its clients spend on its services, it delivers, on average, $100 million in government benefits."[2] The big insult, as we see in scandal after scandal, is not that legislators are for sale, but that they come so cheap, given the rewards to the company. That's another reason why large companies and trade associations are crazy not to get into the lobbying game.

The most notable success for lobbying was that of a "coalition of 60 corporations—including Pfizer, Hewlett-Packard and Altria—that spent $1.6 million in lobbying fees ... to persuade Congress to create a special low tax rate that they could apply to earnings from their foreign operations for one year."[3] As a *Washington Post* story reports, in 2004 "Bush signed into law a bill that reduced the rate to 5 percent, 30 percentage points below the existing levy. More than $300 billion in foreign earnings has since poured into the United States, saving the companies roughly $100 billion in taxes."[4]

Aside from being an enormous (and barely noted) act of corporate welfare for companies that needed it the least, it was also an advertisement to those who did not yet fully get it: that an investment in influencing government could be far more profitable than merely making an innovative product.

The Fear of Not Lobbying

Companies that previously kept themselves aloof from heavy-duty lobbying have now decided that they were obliged, if only in self-defense, to have a cadre of policy influencers on the ground.

For example, Starbucks found it necessary after years of reluctance to hire lobbyists. With over 9,000 stores, Starbucks is exposed more than ever to federal tax, labor, health insurance, and trade policies, all being pushed one way or another by competing interest groups. As a *Wall Street Journal* article put it,

> it's clear that much of the company's future growth will come from overseas. That makes lowering trade barriers with Central America and even far-flung places like Thailand critical issues for the coffee retailer. Double-digit spikes in health-care costs threaten the company's ability to offer medical coverage—a signature employee benefit it extends to even part-time workers. And as the company dips its toe into more sensitive areas, such as coffee-flavored liquor sales, it faces greater regulation.[5]

Given all that, Starbucks cannot afford to ignore what's happening in Washington. In the first big triumph of the lobbying effort, according to the *Wall Street Journal* story, Starbucks managed to get its coffee-roasting operations defined as manufacturing rather than service to preserve a tax break it might otherwise have lost in a new bill.

Further along the lobbying continuum is Wal-Mart. A decade ago, Wal-Mart spent next to nothing on lobbying, based on the precepts of founder Sam Walton not to get entangled with government.[6] But when parts of the U.S.-China trade negotiation cut into Wal-Mart's Asian expansion plans, the firm's management realized it had to use its vast economic power to get the ear of the Washington politicians who were drafting the treaties, regulations, and laws. In 1998, the company hired its first lobbyist. With a taste of success from that venture, Wal-Mart became a bigger player in the lobbying business every year as well as a leading campaign contributor (to Republican candidates).[7] Among the company's objectives, according to a *Wall Street Journal* story, have been to:

- Change the law to allow Wal-Mart to buy banks, so it can offer its own banking services to customers (that one was defeated by the powerful banking lobby)
- Remove of all tariffs on manufactured goods brought into the United States
- Restrict labor organizing at retail stores by banning union activities outside stores
- Set limits on class-action activist suits
- Protect the company against immigration enforcement inspections, which have found undocumented workers (also supporting changes in immigration policy in its favor)[8]

This is quite a shopping list of policy agendas, some legislative and some administrative, and Wal-Mart has made progress on all these goals.

BENDING PUBLIC POLICY

As both the Starbucks and the Wal-Mart examples show, major corporations have seen that they can effectively influence government policy. Moreover, they have found that spending money in that area can have a far higher return than an R&D breakthrough or expanding operations. It's yet another way to get the full benefit of keeping retail prices low, because, in one form or another, your company can be subsidized by the taxpayer. For some companies, the biggest innovations take place in the area of lobbying initiatives.

This chapter can only begin to describe the ways in which public policy is influenced by the biggest companies. We'll look at both well known and less obvious examples. We'll skip the most flagrant law-breaking to consider instead the legal and semilegal methods that corporations are using. The examples are based in the United States, for the most part, but the same can be found in all countries. We'll start with examples involving local governments.

Example One: The Eminent Domain Ploy

One rapidly growing way in which large U.S. corporations are bending the laws to their will is by using local governments' power of eminent domain. Eminent domain, defined in the Fifth Amendment, is the right of government to condemn and take over land (with proper compensation to the owner) for the public good. It has traditionally been used for such public works as highways, schools, bridges, and so forth. Over the last few decades, however, judicial decisions have allowed the law to be applied to almost anything that can be claimed to have an economic benefit for the community.

In this way, the biggest retailers have started to use eminent domain to their own benefit. A *Wall Street Journal* article[9] documents a number of instances of government pushing property owners off their land so that major retailers could move in and build. For example, consider the following:

- Pittsburg, Kansas, used eminent domain to condemn private land so that retailer Home Depot could build a store.
- Port Chester, New York, cleared out its business districts and scores of small retailers to enable Costco and Bed, Bath & Beyond to build megastores.
- Cypress, California, condemned a vacant lot so that Costco could build there.
- North Bergen, New Jersey, condemned a Kmart so that a Home Depot could be built.
- Maplewood, Missouri, condemned 150 homes and businesses and sold the land to Wal-Mart.

Although such big companies decry government oversight and minimum wage hikes, they are more than happy to use government power to get a handout. One observer is quoted in the *Wall Street Journal* article as saying, "They're a new generation of robber barons, like the railroads of the nineteenth century."[10] Like the rail empires of old, retailers are snatching up land intended for "public use," a concept that has been broadened by courts over the last few years.

The article documents a series of dirty tricks and lower-than-appraised compensations for landowners, as the big chains more and more persuade local governments that their own salvation is based on keeping the big companies. Big retailers are likely to abandon that property and run off to the next town if the returns aren't acceptable or the local taxes too onerous. Many towns now have empty superstore buildings with wind-swept parking lots.[11]

The condemnation and takeover game has become the publicly defended modus operandi for some of the big-box companies.[12] Costco, in a letter to stockholders, admitted to making free use of eminent domain or the threat of it in dozens of projects, claiming that if they didn't, then "our competitors for those sites, like Target, Home Depot, Kmart, Wal-Mart, BJ's, Sam's Club, and many others, would take advantage of our reticence."[13] Seen from the perspective of the big retailers, they'd be betraying their stockholders if they did not use the tool of eminent domain. But why do local governments take sides with big retailers against small retailers, homeowners, and property owners?

The old dictum was that "what's good for General Motors is good for the United States"; now the policy might be, "what's good for Wal-Mart or Home Depot is good for the United States, or at least for our town." At least General Motors once provided high-paying, lifetime skilled jobs and developed products people could use.

And retailers are the most conspicuous example of the misuse of eminent domain. As one commentator has asserted, "So-called public purposes these days include headquarters for multinational corporations, sports arenas for national franchises, private research facilities, shopping centers, casinos, private office buildings, etc."[14] Tax breaks and municipal loans often come along with these land grants, which leads us to another pressure big companies can place on local governments, the headquarters gambit.

Example Two: The Headquarters Oligopsony, Playing Hardball

When Philadelphia-based cable giant Comcast decided in 2003 to build a new world headquarters for its fast-growing operations, it wanted a little help. It persuaded the city government of Philadelphia, desperate to hold on to the prestige and jobs generated by a Fortune 100 company, to agree to petition the state government to have a special "Keystone Opportunity Zone" set up in central Philadelphia to locate Comcast's new building.

While the idea of opportunity zones traditionally has been designed to provide tax relief to encourage business and create jobs in depressed city areas, the block to be designated in Philadelphia was decidedly not depressed. It was, in fact, just down the street from the exclusive Four Seasons hotel and surrounded by new skyscrapers hosting law offices and banks. It is among the most expensive commercial properties in the state of Pennsylvania and, except for janitors, security, staff, and kitchen help, offers no jobs to any but the well-dressed and well-educated.

Designating the area as an opportunity zone would allow the company to avoid paying state and local business taxes for up to fifteen years. Of course, the company would spend money associated with building a new skyscraper in the city, and it said that 1,000 or more jobs would be added to the city's tax rolls. It was worth it, said state officials, to back a winner.

Word got out about the deal, and it started a furor over the fact that one of the most profitable companies in the state would get a handout.[15] The opposition of the other media and the citizens was strong, but the key might have been the anger of competing real estate developers. As a result, the state legislature decided not to support the opportunity zone designation.

But all was not lost: The legislature did make several other grants. A $30 million grant went to Comcast's developer, Liberty Property, to pay for site improvements. Comcast also got around $13 million in opportunity grants, job creation tax credits, and job training assistance. The result: everybody was made happy for a mere $50 million or so.

However, as a *Philadelphia Inquirer* story points out, that's an expensive wager on the future of a single company.[16] Pennsylvania, like other states, has rolled the dice before, and has lost big. Pennsylvania spent hundreds of millions to attract Norwegian shipbuilder Kvaerner ASA to the old Philadelphia naval yard, only to find out that Kvaerner was on the brink of bankruptcy and had to be bailed out by another Norwegian company.[17] (The shipyard, after four shaky years, has gotten a longer-term contact that will keep it alive for a few more years.)

In 2004, health care insurer Cigna was being actively courted by New Jersey to move out of Philadelphia and move its 1,500 jobs across the river to Camden.[18] New Jersey offered a package totaling around $100 million, and Pennsylvania and Philadelphia countered with a deal whose terms have not been fully revealed—but we know that the state tossed in at least $10 million in cash and loans plus some tax breaks.

Philadelphia invested millions in buying and clearing land for an urban amusement park called "DisneyQuest," only to see Disney back out and leave a big hole in the ground a few blocks away from the Liberty Bell. (It's jokingly called the DisneyHole.) And so on, and so on. And we're not even talking about the financing of separate football and baseball stadiums for up to half a billion dollars in loan guarantees and fee waivers from the state and city.

Thus, well over a billion Philadelphia and Pennsylvania taxpayer dollars have gone into a series of development projects that have failed to reap the expected awards or have ended up paying companies for what they might have done, in return for hard-to-define benefits. That money has fallen into the hands of big corporations, but it has done little for civic life. And now, when the city and state are having budget problems, when essential infrastructure maintenance work sits undone, and when regular businesses and ordinary taxpayers get no relief, the state and city are still pursuing these phantoms, hoping they'll get it right this time.

As the *Inquirer* article points out, the chances aren't good. "Corporations come and go. Business conditions change. Markets grow and shrink unpredictably. Today's blue-chip is tomorrow's corporate has-been."[19] The problem, of course, was that losing Comcast, then located in the city, would be a dire blow to once-mighty Philadelphia, which today has few enough major corporate headquarters. Comcast could hold the city at ransom, as other corporate leaders and sports owners have, by threatening to move out the suburbs, across the river to New Jersey, or to some Southern state with lower costs of living and no labor issues.

That's because big corporations (and sports franchises) are oligopsonies with respect to a limited resource—their headquarters. There are only a limited number of Fortune 500 headquarters on the market (500, at last count), and a large number of cities, counties, and states bidding to have them located within their borders. And with the Internet, headquarters are less than ever tied to any specific location.

- In 2001, Boeing suddenly moved its headquarters to Chicago, leaving Seattle in the lurch.
- In 2005, International Paper moved its headquarters from Stamford, Connecticut, to Memphis.
- In 2006, car maker Nissan moved its headquarters in 2006 from Los Angeles to Nashville.
- In 2006, PC maker Lenovo (which bought IBM's PC business in 2004) announced it would move its headquarters from suburban New York to North Carolina.

But even more likely are moves after a merger or acquisition. As bank after regional bank, for example, gets swallowed up by the industry giants, cities lose their headquarters. Philadelphia has lost out in the past to a number of such deals, including the loss of Bell Atlantic headquarters after the Verizon merger in 2000. Leaving with these jobs and prestige is the kind of corporate citizenship that supports charities and public institutions. Similar stories can be told of every city.

These "consumers of location" can be very picky and can make demands on their suppliers. They don't need to bluff much—they have all the aces in their hands—and that's why states and cities are willing to make risky bets on gaining a long-term advantage in return for a major shortfall in tax revenue.

Of course, cities, counties, and states fight over all kinds of sites, from auto plants to big-box stores. They load up potential relocations with tax breaks, zoning variations, financing, and other goodies in the hope of beating out the opposition. These are not benefits that they give to smaller, locally derived businesses, which end up footing the bill along with regular taxpayers.

Example Three: Subsidy or Blackmail

In 2004, the generous people of Washington State, through their government, gave a tax-break package of $3.2 billion dollars to Boeing Corporation over 20 years. In return, Boeing agreed not to move production of their latest jetliner out of state.[20] When giant companies threaten, local officials give in to their demands. In this case, the money reportedly saved 800 assembly-line jobs.

Presumably, the numbers said that Washington State would gain more in salary taxes and other business than it would lose. But who ran the numbers? It turns out that the state's consultant in the matter was the consulting arm of accounting giant Deloitte & Touche. It also turns out that Deloitte & Touche earned about $92 million in fees from Boeing in the years when it was consulting with the state of Washington. Of course, both Boeing and Deloitte claim that a firewall was in place between the departments. A *BusinessWeek* article quotes an activist for the public interest group that turned up this connection: "If this isn't a conflict of interest, what is?"[21]

Boeing is not a company that is shy about using its muscle. It's worked with Microsoft to keep receiving major export tax credits from the government when those were threatened in 2004. It was, of course, involved in the scandal of hiring a Pentagon procurement manager who helped arrange cushy deals for Boeing before she left the government. In spite of repeated dubious practices, such as pilfering secret documents from competitor Lockheed Martin and installing known faulty equipment in military helicopters, it still gets a big share of military contracts, partly because its few competitors are little better. Boeing has even been awarded a contract to build the U.S.-Mexico fence, a long leap from building aircraft.

Companies like Boeing are expert in playing off one locale against another to get out of paying taxes. The automakers, for example, both domestic and foreign, are particularly adept at playing off one desperate rural county against another, with companies like Honda and Toyota making conspicuous and prolonged contests out of their site evaluation period. This bidding procedure ensures that big automakers can get a payoff before the first car is built.

> The process typically begins with an announcement like the one from Honda in mid-May 2006 that said the automaker plans to build its sixth North American facility. The new facility's location has not yet been decided, but according to my local newspaper, it is slated to open in 2009 with a capacity of 150,000 vehicles per year.... With the car plant cat out of the bag, we citizens once again get to sit back and watch elected officials trip over each other to entice this facility into their respective state or district.[22]

Indeed Ohio, Illinois, Indiana, and Alabama jumped at the offer and made promises of hundreds of millions of dollars in tax abatements and other fees. Without a national industrial policy, every announced new plant can start an auction that taxpayers pay for. With American manufacturing losing jobs by the millions, those companies that build new plants or expand old ones are, as it were, in the driver's seat. Companies have always opened and closed plants, but now a major consideration is a chance for extra profits.

Example Four: Greasing the Revolving Door

We hate to pick on Boeing again, but it's such a tempting target. The *Wall Street Journal* offers an in-depth analysis of the notorious 2003 U.S. Air Force procurement scandal, involving Boeing's leasing of tanker planes for refueling U.S. jets.[23] At the center of the matter is the "revolving door" that led the principal purchasing officer for the deal to land a high-paying new job at Boeing shortly after the enormously profitable deal was signed. According to the article, it wasn't just Boeing that was interested in hiring the insider knowledge and connections of the government procurement officer. Lockheed Martin and Raytheon, two other defense industry giants, were also jockeying to "buy" her services as well.

Such ethically dubious transitions from the underpaid public sector to the high-salary private sector and the opportunities for corruption that arise have been around since the minutemen ordered their first muskets. But the oligopolization of the defense industry in recent years and the complexity of weapon development have made the potential for abuses greater than ever, as the *Wall Street Journal* article notes:

> Post–Cold War consolidation melded dozens of smaller defense contractors into a handful of giants. As the government modernizes its armed forces, it has become increasingly reliant on contractors such as Boeing to pull together sophisticated weapons systems with products and services from different companies; military officials admit they lack the technical expertise for the job. And because weapons programs cost billions and can take a decade to come to fruition, their official overseers often find their interests closely aligned with the companies they are supposed to police.[24]

As we have seen before, the bigger and fewer the competitors, the more the nominally free market gets distorted. The bigger companies feel the need and have the power to quietly change the rules of the game in their favor. One way to do this is to make their counterparts on the purchasing end realize that a compliant attitude is far more in their long-term interest than an antagonistic one. The little guys don't get such soft treatment. Another journalist notes that a

> federal database on the Internet that lists those companies and individuals that have been banned—either permanently or temporarily—from government work shows hundreds of people and small firms are cut off each year. But major corporations, which get the most money from federal contracts, rarely meet a similar fate.[25]

In the Boeing case, management went beyond the boundaries of prudence and invited public scrutiny. The extravagance of the lease arrangement was not sufficiently complex, so that the bad deal it represented was all too apparent.

Normally, however, the distortion in the system is less easily discovered; here they just went a bit too far in bending the rules. The punishment Boeing got as a corporation—mostly, just a public reprimand—was the equivalent of giving an unruly seven year old a "time out." Boeing is back in the bidding process as if nothing had happened.

Example Five: Oligopolies Get Pension Breaks

The airline and steel oligopolies, among others, got a nice Easter basket from the U.S. government in 2004, as the government passed a new pension law. Under the new law, major companies were allowed to lower their contributions to their pension plans to the tune of $60 billion over the following few years. Even the probusiness *Economist* saw this as a disastrous decision: "Already wobbly companies will thus continue to make pension promises they cannot keep. If anything, the new law will make a bad problem worse."[26] Pensions were hit by low interest rates and the stock market collapse of 2001. They were given a temporary rate adjustment for the required assets in their funds, one that was about to run out.

Pension plans are federally insured, so that, if worse comes to worse, pension funds can dump liability on the government. In this way, once again taxpayers are being asked, indirectly, to subsidize large corporations, many of whom, it has been recently revealed, manage to avoid paying any income taxes at all.

While the legislation is partly trying to give short-term relief to a few embattled industries, the power of the oligopolies in other businesses is such that they have managed to get a long-term government-funded pass on their liabilities. The danger was pointed out by the conservative Heritage Foundation, which sounds the alarm:

> By allowing companies to avoid funding their pension plans' deficits, the new law makes it likely that taxpayers will have to pick up that liability. The sad fact is that many companies that qualify for the funding holiday will be in equally poor financial shape in 2006. The delay is likely to cause these plans to accrue even higher funding deficits. Moreover, once the companies submit their even more underfunded plans to PBGC [Pension Benefit Guaranty Corporation], that agency will be further down the road toward an inevitable taxpayer-funded, multibillion-dollar bailout.[27]

It's a two-pronged attack—the companies renege on their debt to former workers, and they make other taxpayers pick up a new financial obligation, even while government officials warn that taxpayers' own long-term Social Security coverage is in doubt.

Example Six: Multinationals Versus the National Interest

We live in a world where corporations are getting less and less identified with nation states. Public policy is often made on the presumption that an

American bank, like Citigroup, is somehow "ours" in a way that a British bank like Bank of Scotland or a Swiss bank like UBS is not. But the days when such national banks or any other corporations were agents of their native country are becoming more and more remote.

Cross-border mergers, a steady internationalization of the management of top companies, and an increasing dependence on non-U.S. sales, investments, and operations mean that even the most all-American companies are starting to have more employees and investments outside the United States than inside.

Indeed, being too closely associated with the United States (KFC, McDonald's) can open companies up to boycotts and property damage. American foreign policy and military moves can lead to problems for U.S.-identified companies operating outside the country. In 2006, the U.S. government drafted large corporations to help in relief efforts in Pakistan and Central America, in part to improve U.S. image abroad, but the motives rarely are simple patriotism.[28] For the companies that are involved, one article notes, "U.S. multinational companies have preferred to emphasize the length and extent of their presence in overseas markets rather than their American-ness."

About the program in Pakistan, Citigroup CEO Sanford Weill was quoted as saying, "I think companies are realizing that we all have to be salesmen for America and not just sit back and rely on the government."[29] In the end, using big U.S. companies to supplement foreign aid programs seems bound to backfire. For many years, U.S. foreign policy has been constrained by economic interests, and the biggest companies have their say even when other principles may be involved, and this is to some extent independent of administrations. For example, our interests (and those of major U.S. companies) in China (manufacturing and treasury note holdings), Saudi Arabia (oil), and Nigeria (oil) have muffled U.S. concerns about human rights in those countries.

Having the biggest companies work as agents of the United States abroad will require further payback in terms of shaping foreign policy. And what's good for Citigroup and Pfizer may often be at odds with what is good policy for the country. It may come in the form of a quiet veto rather than a positive initiative, but in the end, the line between what the U.S. government wants and what these market-dominating companies want must get blurred. There's always a quid pro quo.

Example Seven: Getting a Seat at the Table

One of the reasons for building a market-dominating company is the ability to be in the room when the big decisions are being made. One way of doing this is by having your company's representative on a standards-setting body. Despite protestations of abhorrence for government control, oligopolies love government control when they have a major hand in dictating it. Strong oligopolies have the money and thus the political capital to get the ears of government officials, and that access puts them in a different category from smaller entities. The big companies regularly get to participate in writing the rules, something consumer and employee groups rarely get. The new rules are often written to inhibit small competitors and to release barriers to big companies, warding off the threat of disruption.

Take genetically modified (GM) foods. Many of us have mixed feeling about GM foods. Some days, it seems they will poison the food supply and the environment, imperiling it through monoculture; other days, it seems that, if managed in moderation, they might help to alleviate some hunger and cut down on the use of pesticides. Certainly, we hope that our government will make wise decisions in regulating their use.

But when the Codex Alimentarius Commission, a United Nations group that sets standard for labeling GM foods, met in Ottawa in 1999, guess who was sitting the table? That group, which runs under the World Health Organization (WHO) and the Food and Agriculture Organization (FAO), is supposed to protect consumers. According to the *Toronto Star*, however, the U.S. and Canadian delegations were chockablock full with representatives from Big Food.

> The Canadian delegation includes six government representatives and 13 non-governmental delegates. Industry representatives fill nine of those 13 non-governmental spots. The companies include Nestlé Canada, Procter & Gamble, Bestfoods Canada, Monsanto Canada, and trade organizations representing industry giants.
>
> The U.S. delegation includes 14 non-government advisers, 10 of whom represent multinational food companies or their trade organizations and consultants who help get the products to market. The companies include Nestlé USA, Bestfoods, Procter & Gamble, and Mead Johnson and Co., maker of infant formula.[30]

By contrast, only four representatives of smaller organic food companies and farmers were included in the two delegations. And guess what the position of the two delegations was:

> Canada and the United States both oppose mandatory labeling that would tell consumers whether the products they are buying have been genetically modified or are so-called novel foods created by biotechnology.[31]

By dominating the North American delegation, the Big Food companies made sure that there would be no world consensus on labeling GM foods, even though, for example, irradiated foods and foods with additives are so labeled. They have more than a voice in the market, they have a voice in how consumers and workers are to be protected (or not) by their governments.

That's just one example of the way in which the biggest companies and their trade associations are called in to "advise" when policy is made. The beef industry was given major access to U.S. Department of Agriculture (USDA) policy in setting "mad-cow disease" policy, while consumer groups were often shut out. It's no coincidence that the Big Beef companies are major political contributors and that key USDA personnel are the beneficiaries of the revolving door.[32]

Similarly, U.S. trade advisory committees are dominated by the Pfizers, Wal-Marts, and McDonald's of the world. Scientists on FDA panels are often consultants hired by the drug companies whose drugs they are reviewing. And the White House gets most of its advice on energy policy through meetings with Big Oil executives.

In countless other ways, oligopolies and their trade groups write legislation, set standards, determine minimum wage, set tax policies, and persuade governments to modify health and safety standards, all in the interest of encouraging business. In return, politicians receive campaign contributions, speaker fees, and other benefits, things that the small businesses that compete with the oligopolies can't afford.

Example Eight: A Seat at the Table, a Hand on the Pen

But getting a seat at the table is mere child's play. The really influential companies get a hand on the pen, "helping" busy legislators and administrators and their staffs draft new laws and write guidelines and regulations. They are especially helpful in areas where the law is confusing and needs expert advice. What better experts than the companies that are in that very industry? As one writer put it in 2005, "There are no restraints now; business groups and lobbyists are going crazy—they're in every room on Capitol Hill writing the legislation."[33]

This scenario is illustrated in a *New York Times* article that shows pharmaceutical companies working on state health regulatory boards so that they mandate their drugs for patients—making it hard for doctors to prescribe an alternative, even when the alternative is cheaper and equally or more effective.[34] Ten major drug companies, for example, used such tactics to make sure that state mental hospitals and Medicaid adopted their drugs in preference to others. Notable among these drugs were new antipsychotic drugs made by Johnson & Johnson in preference to generic drugs whose patents have run out. These tactics were recently brought to light by a Pennsylvania lawsuit, according to the *Times* story.

> Ten drug companies chipped in to underwrite the initial effort by Texas officials to develop the guidelines. Then, to spread the word, Johnson & Johnson, Pfizer and possibly other companies paid for meetings around the country at which officials from various states were urged to follow the example of Texas.[35]

The companies apparently flew various state commissioners to New Orleans, wined and dined them, and paid others generous fees for speaking at company-sponsored seminars. It's still controversial, according to the article, whether the new drugs are that much better than the older, cheaper ones. But one thing is certain: there's a large amount of money in the market for antipsychotic drugs, around $6.5 billion in 2003.

The Texas guidelines, drafted by a government agency with private sector "help" set out the acceptable pharmacology not only for psychosis, but also for schizophrenia, depression, attention deficit disorder, and bipolar disorder. The drug companies involved reply that they are only trying to improve treatments based on their extensive research. They characterize their task as educational only. But there's a pretty thin line here between education and forcing sales, especially when state and federal governments can't do the extensive testing required and when the drug companies commission their own tests for efficacy. And there's really no counterweight, either from neutral researchers or less-wealthy generic competitors.

Influencing government decisions in any health field is becoming increasingly critical for drug companies' financial health. As more and more doctors and hospitals are put in the position of simply diagnosing a disease and prescribing an "acceptable" drug, the drug companies will use their money and influence to make sure they are one of those acceptable drugs. The persuadability of underfunded state health commissions makes them easy prey for the drug companies, and when they act in concert, as they did in Texas, they can safely divvy up the pie and jointly unseat generic drugs.

There's a zero-sum game at work here, too. As Medicare and Medicaid funds are being cut by the federal government, every extra dollar spent on nonpatented medicines instead of on cheaper, effective generics is one less dollar for nursing care, doctor's fees, and hospital bills.

Example Nine: Too Big to Fail

The "too big to fail" issue also comes into play. The government in 2005 backed off a fine for Big Four accounting and auditing firm KPMG, which created clearly illegal tax shelters for some of its clients and made many millions doing it. The Justice Department decided not to pursue major damages against the company, which will have to make reparations, lest it create another Arthur Andersen–type failure. That's a signal that the big companies will now get different treatment for their sins than small firms could expect.

That point was put forth in an Associated Press story:

> "In the way that 'too big to fail' became an unofficial doctrine of policy toward corporations, 'too concentrated to indict' has become a moniker for the accounting industry," suggested John C. Coffee, a law professor at Columbia University. "It's a strange kind of immunity" for KPMG, he said. "While the prosecutors in principle wield the club of potential indictment, the firm knows that being put in the criminal dock is unlikely and thereby gains a certain leverage in the negotiations," Coffee said.[36]

The same doctrine holds true for top defense companies, including Raytheon, Lockheed Martin, L-3, Halliburton, Northrop Grumman, and (inevitably) Boeing. No matter how many cases of incompetence, corporate espionage, and outright fraud these companies may be party to, they never are severely reprimanded and never are in serious danger of being cut off. There are few replacements for these companies, and they are as likely to have strikes against them as well. Likewise, failing airlines were propped up after 9/11, and the government seems determined to make sure that Ford and GM survive. Smaller companies need not apply.

TO SUM UP

These examples could be extended ad nauseam, and they could be applied to every industry. Almost everything government bodies do has a monetary impact on some big business, whether it's the allocation of funds to build a bridge or signing a free trade pact with Chile. Even inaction, such as the lax enforcement of some regulation or the omission of a phrase from a bill, can be worth millions to companies.

Although, occasionally, a smaller company, through personal connections, gets a few scraps thrown its way out the back door (as in the 2005 "Duke" Cunningham bribery scandal), it is the biggest companies that can walk in the front door and pull up a chair. These companies' executives, as we have shown, have learned how to play the system.

7 / Convergence, Choice, and Consolidation

WHAT IS THE DIFFERENCE BETWEEN CELL PHONES made by Nokia and those made by Motorola? What features do Canon copiers have that Ricoh copiers don't? How different is an overnight stay in a Marriott hotel as opposed to a Westin hotel? Which brand washes your clothing cleaner, Procter & Gamble's Tide or Unilever's All? Which is the better way to send a package, FedEx, UPS, or DHL?

For most of us who aren't opinionated specialists, big fans of a specific brand, or writers of marketing copy, the answer is either "not much" or "not sure." And the same can be applied to thousands of other consumer experiences. In many areas, products have reached near parity. That's not to deny the real differences between the handling on a Toyota Camry and on a Ford Taurus, or between the taste of Heinz and Hunt's ketchups. But it's almost certain that the gap is narrowing.

Competitive differences tend to narrow over time, as they must when companies are trying to keep up with better selling rivals. When markets are dominated by a few companies, the consequence is a notable sameness among the big players and their products. Erstwhile competitors become increasingly similar, in strategy and in their impact on society. We might call this a side effect of competition for market dominance, because it is not directly part of the high-level financial struggles that motivate the market but is almost incidental to the bigger issues. Nevertheless, it may have a direct impact on our daily life.

CONVERGENCE

Imitation is inevitable in businesses, big and small alike. If the tavern down the street starts to draw more customers by offering free food at happy hour, then other bars in the area inevitably follow suit. If one dry cleaner in town offers three-hour service and gets a competitive advantage, chances are that others are likely to do the same, or even offer one-hour service. Big companies are even better and faster at watching and learning from the competition.

As industries consolidate, the companies in them tend to get more and more alike. This tendency toward convergence is an axiom of the game of domination. The #1 player in an industry sets the tone and establishes the best practices, and the rest follow. But the leader also looks nervously over its shoulder, ready to adopt any competitive breakthroughs that might threaten its position. Best Buy, the electronics leader, is clearly mirrored by #2 Circuit City, and vice versa, as prices, policies, products, and layouts run in tandem. Dell and Hewlett-Packard are engaged in a similar dance. Hershey's keeps an eye on Mars and Nestlé, and they in turn watch the others for any hint of a breakthrough approach or product category.

Convergence tends to grind away at companies that were once very different. Over time Target and Tesco become more like Wal-Mart, TV networks become interchangeable, Burger King becomes more like McDonald's, Airbus more like Boeing, Bank of America and HSBC more like Citigroup. After all, if another company is beating yours, you want to find and use their secrets, their "best practices."

In an economy dominated by oligopolies, convergence speeds up. The few players in an oligopoly tend in most ways to become just like each other. This may seem wrongheaded; surely there's no competitive advantage in being just like your biggest rivals; after all, doesn't originality give one company its distinction and advantage?

Certainly, originality can be a plus. But as oligopolies tighten, rivals have the means and interest to match every competitor's breakthrough. The comparative advantage of any original move is short-lived, readily imitated. As we have seen in Chapter 4, real, disruptive innovation can create problems for bigger companies. Recognizing and adopting useful, bite-size innovations, however, is something many market-leading companies are really expert at.

And when companies are joined through merger and acquisition, their identifying characteristics are quickly worn away, even though that is rarely the announced intention. This happens with national companies that lose their corporate culture after a merger—either the acquirer (Hewlett-Packard's "HP Way") or the acquiree (Ben & Jerry's "caring capitalism"). In every case, despite the best advice of merger advisors and the promises of management, sooner or later the culture gets homogenized when companies are acquired. This is especially true when the culture of a small entrepreneur is ingested by a large corporation.

Such homogenization is particularly noticeable in multinational companies. The combination of Daimler-Benz and Chrysler made both operations less distinct.[1] Multinational convergence is often compounded by the adoption of a common language (English) that is not native for many executives: how else can Finns talk with Brazilians or Chinese?[2] Many multinational companies tend to lose their original national identity or local flavor. At the highest levels, they become denizens of a homogenized worldwide MBA culture.[3]

All kinds of forces bring companies together in a kind of gravitational pull. What follows are some ideas on how convergence inside an oligopoly happens.

Personnel: The Same Faces

Oligopolies hire one another's executives. Over and over again, a successful vice president of one company, perhaps passed over from the top spot, is lured away by a close competitor for a higher position and higher pay. Companies #2 and #3 in any business want to have the magic of #1 rub off, and in an industry like television where ratings are strictly measured and frequently changing, the game of musical chairs goes on endlessly. But even in more staid industries like banking and insurance, the top lieutenants at company A are often picked to head company B before company B's own aspirants. Further down the line, a mid-level management job at a Microsoft or Procter & Gamble frequently converts into a higher-level job at some lesser competitor.

Following are a few examples out of the thousands of such personnel moves each year:

- In 2003, vaccine maker Chiron named as CEO the former GlaxoSmithKline president of pharmaceuticals international.
- In 2004, Sirius satellite radio hired the former Viacom president of entertainment and sports as CEO.
- In 2005, Safeway hired Wal-Mart's CFO of international operations to become senior vice president of internal audit.
- In 2006, Amazon.com brought in a Microsoft senior vice president as a senior vice president.
- In an extreme example, PepsiCo hired Irene Rosenfeld, president of Kraft's North American operations, as CEO of its Frito-Lay operation in 2004; in 2006 Kraft hired her back as CEO.

And so on. It makes sense, of course, to hire experienced senior personnel with industry experience who want to take the next step in their careers. The result is a remarkable homogeneity in executive personnel between companies in an oligopoly. The practices and the values of different companies tend to resemble each other over time. Companies fail to retain a special character or esprit. The idea that "that's the way we've always done it here" gives way to "that's the way my former, more successful company does it."

A side effect of this is an artificially small pool of executive talent that leads to higher executive pay. Certain people are singled out as potential CEOs and COOs by hiring committees on corporate boards, and most have the same characteristics and background as the current executives.[4] It has been argued that it is in the interest of such hiring committees (made up of top executives from other companies) to maintain that scarcity, as its affects their own compensation.[5] In any case, the process ends up with similar execs with similar approaches.

Product Convergence

Someone once compared the desperately conformist organization to a group of ten year olds playing soccer.[6] You can always tell where the ball is because it is surrounded by everyone on the field. No one stakes out a position; they all just converge on the ball, making for lots of inept play. Likewise, companies in an oligopoly, once they identify a trend (often innovated by a smaller competitor), spend much time and money in glomming on to the new trend. So Vanilla Coke generates Vanilla Pepsi, *Survivor* spawns a plethora of similar "reality" shows, and all foods go from "low fat" to "low carb" overnight. When one trend cools another takes over (those same "low-carb" foods are replaced with 100-calorie servings or organic versions).[7]

That's why all car companies offer essentially the same mix of similar-looking sedans, SUVs, and pickups, and now even hybrids, and the ability to distinguish a Ford from a Toyota at a glance, once so easy, has become quite hard. It's also why CNN and MSNBC look and sound more and more like Fox News. It's why if you were teleported into a random CVS, Walgreens, or Rite Aid drugstore, you'd have no idea which one it was, as the products available and the store layout would be essentially identical.

Such imitation and trend-following have always been a major part of the business world. Borrowing someone else's hot idea, just this side of violating patent and copyright laws, is a lot easier than coming up with your own. An idea can reach the "tipping point": yesterday it was nowhere, today it is everywhere. And modern corporations are better placed than ever to retool themselves to meet the new need.

Moreover, in our age of oligopoly, companies seem to be far more highly attuned than ever to this process of product trend chasing. With enormous and immediate numerical feedback, executives are more aware than ever of the minimal variations in demand for products and services, both theirs and their competitors. Every slight advantage from the opposition brings a counterplan, usually to do the same thing that seemingly gave the opposition the lift. Through constant microadjustments, divergent competitors offer increasingly similar products. Any breakout is immediately pursued by all the market players—again, within the limits of the patent and copyright laws.

Common Methods

A similar process happens in the area of business methods. Take, for example, the science of site location. From a haphazard, by-the-gut process of locating retail branches, over the last few years a whole new methodology for finding optimal store locations has arisen. At first, only a few market leaders like McDonald's or Wal-Mart put the time and money into perfecting this approach. Now it's unthinkable that any retailer beyond a mom-and-pop would not call on the same methods—to the extent they can afford them—as McDonald's and Wal-Mart. Their competitors therefore end up making the same kinds of choices, driving up the price of the most desirable locations even further.[8]

Similarly, the publicity rollouts of big studio movies follow a schedule and breadth (from the gossip column stories to the onslaught of television ads on youth-oriented shows and the inevitable stars appearing on the *Today Show*, *Larry King*, and *The Daily Show*) that has developed over time, but now it is totally rigid and predictable, so much so that the campaign schedule for any given movie could be exchanged with that of any other with only trivial modifications.[9]

That's why MasterCard and Visa are virtually identical in the way they work, and why American Express is desperately trying to follow their lead. It's why all retail banks seem like minor variations of each other, even to the same meaningless ads that trumpet how much they care about their customers. It's why Borders and Barnes & Noble bookstores have coffee bars that feel just like Starbucks outlets, and it's why they all serve pretty much the same drinks. It's why all direct mail looks the same, and it's why all online shopping experiences feel similar to Amazon's. In each of these cases, the imitation of these similar business practices may be executed more or less effectively, but they all reflect the way in which it's not just products but ways of doing business that converge.

Joint Ventures

Another of the areas where competitors come close together is in joint ventures. These are all over the map. Petroleum giants Shell and ExxonMobil work together to manufacture and sell lubricants and other chemicals. Film studios regularly take on some of the funding for other studios' films. Steel giant Mittal works with rivals Nippon Steel and Shanghai Baosteel. Cingular was owned jointly by BellSouth and SBC (AT&T), until they were all the same company. Rivals Boeing and Lockheed Martin work together to develop military space vehicles. Comcast, Time Warner Cable, and Cox Communications, the three biggest cable television companies, are in the cell phone service business together. Hitachi and General Electric build nuclear energy plants in a joint venture. Toshiba and Canon, competitors in many areas, work jointly on flat-screen display technology. NEC and Panasonic, frequent rivals, work together on cell phone technology development.

Working on joint ventures requires that two companies mingle personnel, products, and methods. It fuses a common interest that has to persist even when the two companies are strong competitors in other areas. It's a fast way to turn enemies into "friendly enemies."

It also creates murky borderline issues. Antitrust regulators try to detect when cooperation in the joint venture spills over into an area in which two firms should be competing strenuously. The Federal Trade Commission (FTC), for example, has elaborate guidelines for what is and is not acceptable behavior in a joint venture.[10] But attempting to fix a firewall between what joint partners can discuss (related to the venture) and what they can't discuss (such as the prices and costs of the rest of their business) is no easy task. Surely, for legal purposes, the written correspondence and witnessed conversations bend over backward to preserve the rules; but over a few drinks or on the golf course, who knows what might get discussed? And if these joint ventures don't end in direct collusion, they certainly allow further transfer of business methods and, therefore, greater homogenization.

Trade Associations

The same holds true for trade associations, a place where ostensibly competitive companies are joined to work for common goals. Associations like the Recording Industry Association of America, the Motion Picture Association of America, the National Cable Television Association, the American Petroleum Institute, and the Grocery Manufacturers of America (with such members as Kraft, General Mills, and Kellogg's) basically are lobbying groups that fight for legislative advantages for their members, and sometimes only for their biggest members.

In some cases, these associations can be channels for price-fixing among the top competitors, or for setting anticompetitive policies that exclude other companies. But even without criminal complicity, they make oligopoly executives aware of the shared interests among similar companies, even if they compete with them in the market.

A small but compelling example of this tendency was seen in the case of the now-disbanded Model Managers Association, an association of top modeling agencies (such as Ford Models, Wilhelmina Model Agency, Next Model Management, and Elite Model Management). According to a *Wall Street Journal* story, these companies were involved in a kickback and price-fixing scandal, keeping their commissions high and locking out lower-priced rivals.[11]

These top agencies were in an oligonomy position, abetted by a trade group. They gained in both directions. They are the main supplier of the best models so they have a powerful oligopoly position in relation to the ad agencies and clothing manufacturers. On the other side, they are about the only way for models to get bookings, an oligopsony. Conspiracy, price-fixing, and illegal kickbacks are the frosting on the cake.

They are also a good example of our principle of "friendly enemies" within an oligopoly. According to the *Wall Street Journal* article, insiders were surprised that the principals could collude in this way, "because the firms' managers were always feuding."[12]

This is an extreme case, perhaps, but again the collaboration between rivals even if innocent can't help but lead to convergence in ways of thinking and conducting business.

Market Discipline

All publicly held companies are under intense scrutiny by the same analysts and investor community. When these companies see a competitor gain an advantage, the pressure to conform to the practices of its rival is intense. That pressure can be felt in terms of executives, products, and methods. If a company's numbers are lagging and a rival is getting ahead with an innovative feature or method, the external pressure to follow suit is powerful.

Mergers and Acquisitions

Of course, after a merger deal, convergence is taken to its logical conclusion, as the methods and culture of one company are subsumed into another. There may be a mix, but that is rare. While the acquirer tries to reassure the acquirees that nothing will change, it inevitably will. First, the accounting systems have to be standardized, then the IT systems, then the HR functions (hiring, benefits, promotions policies). Finally, all the methods and culture are standardized. In this way, employees used to innovative or eccentric benefits policies at one company often see those add-ons disappear after a takeover.

HP has so totally integrated Compaq that it's hard to remember that Compaq ever existed, as, indeed, Compaq previously absorbed Digital Equipment. Disney recently transformed smaller movie studio Miramax, though the idea was that Miramax would act "semi-independently."[13] No trace of Pillsbury exists except for a few brand names since its 2001 merger with General Mills.

When organic yogurt maker Stonyfield Farm was bought out by Danone, the pressure was on for the company's management to maintain growth of 20 to 40 percent a year. This is at war with the original ideals of the company, as Stonyfield Farm has been forced to change and speed up its practices. For example, instead of just working with local dairy farmers, the company has been forced to import powdered organic milk from New Zealand, due to a lack of organic milk in the United States.[14] Its practices are evolving into those of a global corporation—it's becoming more like its parent.

The pressures to converge are inexorable. What is fascinating, though it's a subject we can't begin to cover in this book, is the way in which these conformist, converging industries have learned to keep from being overturned, for the most part, by disruptive rivals who can really adapt more rapidly to changing technology and fashions.

Groupthink

Given all these convergence pressures, it's almost inevitable that companies in an oligopoly tend to engage in groupthink. Groupthink is the trend of a group (here, executives) to share converging ideas, whether or not they make sense in the real world. This can lead to a business strategy of adapting to identified competitors, rather than to the underlying needs of the market and fundamental changes in technology.

The recording industry's disastrous reaction to the threat of digital music is an example of bad adaptation through groupthink—it's surprising that none of the big companies has really found a new approach. It's almost as certain that the movie, television, and book publishing oligopolies are starting on the same route that has bedeviled newspapers. The U.S. automobile business engaged in its own groupthink as it lost more and more ground to foreign competitors. The residential real estate industry is in decline as it loses ground to Internet sales.

Groupthink is also dangerous financially. The dot-com bubble was a disaster not only for many private investors, but spelled near-doom for companies that bought too far into the hype (especially Time Warner). We've talked earlier (in Chapter 3) about the feeding frenzy that can take place in the merger and acquisitions sector, when the fear of being left behind is greater than the consideration of the intrinsic worth of any deal. Potential bubbles in private equity and in new Web 2.0 companies (think YouTube) are sparked by similar groupthink.

VARIETY

From the consumer side, one of the biggest objections to convergence among a few companies in any market is lack of choice. A market with only a few converging vendors might tend to be limited, in which only the most dominant tastes are served. In the terms of *The Long Tail*, this means featuring only the biggest hits at the expense of niche markets.[15]

We see this in the movie industry, where the approach of the big studios and big movie chains traditionally has meant that most films, and certainly the most available films, fall into a few well-defined categories starring a few well-known stars. Minority tastes are shunted aside by the law of the market. Likewise, the typical dominance of certain food processing companies used to mean that your choices for breakfast cereal, cookies, and ice cream could be severely limited by the marketing judgments and complacency of the big companies. Such a situation would be frustrating for consumers and would have the potential to provoke a reaction. Our society demands variety, if for no other reason than to give us a feeling of power as shoppers.

Pseudovariety

One technique retail oligopolies use is to flood the shelves with a *pseudovariety* of similar products made in almost exactly the same way, so that minor vendors that offer real variety are elbowed out of the market. The beer industry is a great example of this trend.

In one episode of the animated television show *The Simpsons*, Homer Simpson takes a tour of the local "Duff" brewery. What we see (and Homer doesn't) is one master pipe that divides into three pipes to supply three enormous vats, one labeled Duff Regular, a second Duff Light, and a third Duff Dry. The point is clear: these three varieties (and we might add Duff Ice and Old Duff) are essentially the same. They represent not real variety, but the illusion of variety—that is, pseudovariety. One or two ingredients are changed, but products with significant differences are crowded off the shelves.[16]

So while no supermarket, convenience store, or other retailer is likely to fill more than a few yards of the shelf space dedicated to beer sales with regular Budweiser, it is more than happy to include a full range—Bud Light, Bud Dry, Bud Ice, Bud Ice Light, Michelob, Michelob Light, Michelob Dry, Michelob Ultra, Busch, Busch Light, Busch Ice, Natural Light, and Natural Ice, all from the same company, Anheuser-Busch, which owns a little more than 50 percent of the U.S. beer market. These seemingly distinct beers fill up many yards of shelf space.

Any European beer drinker (and plenty of Americans) would find little difference in taste between any of these brands.[17] These are all products from the same Anheuser-Busch vats, and they are all in same style of American lager.

If this shelf coverage isn't enough, look at the brands of the other oligopoly competitors:

- Miller (almost 30 percent of the domestic beer market) sells Miller High Life, Miller High Life Lite, Miller High Life Ice, Miller Lite, Miller Lite Ice, Miller Genuine Draft, Miller Genuine Draft Light, Miller Ice House, Milwaukee Best, Milwaukee Best Light, and Milwaukee Best Ice.
- Coors (10 percent of the market) offers Coors Light, Original Coors, Coors Arctic Ice, Coors Arctic Ice Light, Coors Extra Gold, and Coors Dry, along with Molson beer.
- Pabst Brewing Company (the fourth major American beer manufacturer) offers similar beers: Pabst Blue Ribbon, Stroh's, Stroh's Light, Schlitz, Old Milwaukee, Old Milwaukee Ice, Old Milwaukee Light, Schmidt's, Schaffer, Schaeffer Light, and others. In fact, most of the Pabst beers are brewed under contract by Miller, a division of worldwide brewer SABMiller.

These beers all represent two basic categories of all the kinds of beers available—namely, American-style lager and American-style light beer, a watered-down version of the same. Although taste varies, these variations are small. In contrast, The Great American Beer Festival, an annual contest, offers 56 distinct categories of beer brewed in the United States by small firms, among which are varieties of porter, stout, wheat beers, bitter, brown ale, pale ale, bock, pilsner, and fruit beers. Granted none of these are popular drinks in the United States, but they hardly have a chance, elbowed off the shelves by a mass of close variations on the same theme.[18]

Once all these American lagers and light beers are on the shelves, they are complemented with a few real (though mild) variations of Anheuser-Busch brands as well: Michelob Golden Draft, Michelob Golden Draft Light, Michelob Classic Dark, and a few others. The other manufacturers offer a few similar products. And several microbrewery labels are owned or sponsored by one of the big three.

But the main result of this situation is the false appearance of enormous diversity and bounty, but the reality is an oligopoly of a few companies with little variety in taste, but wide variety in packaging. The shelf space is occupied, and free choice, which seems unlimited, is in fact restricted.

The pseudovariety of most beer retailers causes few grumbles. Consumers are free to choose, but their choices are focused on small differences.

Another example of pseudovariety is in toothpaste. There are two major companies that dominate the toothpaste shelves, Colgate-Palmolive and Procter & Gamble (Crest). Check almost any retailer that sells toothpaste and the vast majority of tubes (more than 75 percent where I have looked) will be variations on Colgate or Crest, with a few tubes of Pepsodent, Arm & Hammer, and perhaps a little space for organic toothpaste specialist Tom's of Maine (recently bought by Colgate).

This situation is perfectly captured in a diatribe by entrepreneur Jay Cross on his Web site Internet Time Blog.[19]

> When I was growing up, shopping for toothpaste was a no-brainer: Grab a tube of Crest. These days my drugstore in North Berkeley carries twenty-four kinds of Crest toothpaste ... : peroxide, baking soda, sensitive, tartar-fighting, cavity-protection, dual-action, multi-care whitening, cinnamon gel, fresh citrus gel, extreme herbal mint, plus scope, or rejuvenating effects. Unfortunately, Procter & Gamble doesn't make any Crest that's just plain toothpaste.

Whatever adventurousness you might want to express, whatever desire to nonconform, is made all the more difficult by the illusion that these companies are offering such a wide variety of choice that we can express ourselves without risk. The lack of real choice is disguised, softened by the seeming cornucopia of choices.

Choice and Oligopolies

Psychologist Barry Schwartz, in his book *The Paradox of Choice*, makes a convincing case that the growing number of choices in the market and in life has made people generally less happy, and this may well be correlated with the increases in depression in First World countries.[20] Although a growth in choices is empowering up to a point, people increasingly are tangled up in issues of remorse, disappointment, empty status-seeking, and an ability to be content with good enough.

As Schwartz points out, psychological studies have shown that, contrary to rational expectations, the ability to choose among scores of options makes people either avoid any choice or regret the choice they do make:

> A large number of options may discourage customers because it forces an increase in the effort that goes into making a decision. So consumers decide not to decide, and don't buy the product. Or if they do, the effort that the decision requires detracts from the enjoyment derived from the results.[21]

Then why do companies persist in adding variations of the same product in such a way to make choices hard? Why does Danone offer so many flavors of yogurt, Nabisco (Kraft) so many types and sizes of cookies, and Procter & Gamble so many variations of Crest toothpaste, and Anheuser-Busch so many equivalent beer varieties? If Schwartz is right, then these companies are making many of their customers more unhappy with the prospect of choosing the right products and less content with the choices they eventually make. Yet clearly these companies' marketing departments are not run by dummies. Several reasons explain why they are willing to risk trying the patience of their customers.

First, there is the issue of controlling shelf space. If jam maker Smucker's doesn't come out with a wide array of flavors, sizes, and approaches (low sugar, no sugar, just fruit), the company risks losing shelf space to a competitor who will offer boysenberry or black cherry preserves, even if the majority of buyers only want strawberry or raspberry. Defense of shelf space is a key motive.

Second, companies with well-established brands have a big advantage when shoppers are fatigued. That's when they are more likely to reach for something that looks familiar rather than shop carefully by looking at price and specific qualities. Straying from the biggest brands (almost all owned by oligopolies) takes work, a clear mind, and the kind of effort few people are up for more than a few times a day.

Third, the blanket coverage discourages new rivals, even serving as a barrier to entry. Suppose you're a local producer of apple juice who wants to break into the market. You (with luck) get an appointment with the buyer for a supermarket chain with your own sugar-free, organic apple juice, a great product. The buyer tells you the following:

> How can you compete against Mott's (a division of beverage powerhouse Cadbury Schweppes), which has two varieties that you'll have to battle with: Mott's Natural and Mott's Plus Light. There's also Martinelli's, a midsize, established privately held cider maker, which sells its Unfiltered Apple Juice, Organic Apple Juice, and Organic Sparkling Cider brands. Finally, there's Earth's Best, a division of major food producer Heinz, which also sells its own brand of organic apple juice aimed at children. That's three major vendors with some ability to promote their products. And that's not counting all the varieties of nonorganic apple juice sold by well-established companies. I don't need or want you. My advice, forget about it.

The calculation is that the benefits derived from keeping out rivals, grabbing more space on the shelves, and getting the benefit of throw-up-the-hands default purchases far outweigh the customer's distress and dissatisfaction and the wastefulness of carrying more brands than will sell on a regular basis.

If consolidation and convergence take variety out of a market, the survivors are eager to give consumers a sense of competition for their attention by a seemingly endless set of choices. In the end, we suspect that so much choice causes most consumers to throw up their hands, grab a case of Bud Lite and any kind of Colgate toothpaste, and head for the checkout.

REDEFINING THE LANDSCAPE

An even more particular way in which convergence has social effects is the way that market-dominating companies have transformed the landscape, both urban and suburban. In a way, every store or shop and its signage is an advertisement for itself. And driving along a suburban road has become as much an advertising experience as watching TV—even more so, since there is almost no relief from the golden arches, the LensCrafters, and the Olive Gardens—and you can't fast forward (or you'll risk getting pulled over by the police).

In the United States, the streets and highways are defined by the presence of large, national or international companies in all the key locations. The cityscape of any American downtown is a series of Starbucks, Barnes & Nobles, major banks, Gaps, and so on, with other smaller local companies on the margin (on the side streets). In the suburbs, this is even more evident: Safeways, major gas stations, Wal-Marts, Marriotts, KFCs, Home Depots, Burger Kings, Honda dealers, and their like define all the focal points in the landscape. Their frequency reaffirms their dominance.[22]

None of this is a surprise. The largest chains are served by active real estate departments that are determined to secure all the key locations in every town, the ones likeliest to draw traffic. These companies have imposed a uniform landscape across the country, so that the suburbs of Dallas look almost exactly like those of Detroit, and where the uniqueness of even a New York or a San Francisco is challenged by the all-too-familiar sequence of national chain stores.

As national oligopolies get bigger, they impose a sameness that is overwhelming. Anyone who has done a lot of business travel knows how all the airports, all the hotels, and all the restaurants tend to blend together. Business travelers who zip between such once-unique cities like Miami, San Francisco, Boston, and Chicago find that their experiences in all those places tend to merge despite the seeming uniqueness of the locations.

In Europe, this process is at a much earlier stage. Yes, there are Total gas stations, Carrefour hypermarkets, Renault dealers, and BNP Paribas bank branches throughout France, not to mention the ubiquitous McDonald's, but they are far more likely to share prime space with a local café, a pastry shop, a local bookstore, or an independent clothing store.

But even in Europe, this trend is changing rapidly. More and more the main streets in all towns, including the small, historic ones like Perugia, Italy, or Arles, France, which used to house only independent clothing stores, shoe repair workshops, and the like, are now virtually indistinguishable. You can walk down the street in Brussels, Milan, or Budapest and likely see Benetton (Italy), Sisley (French), Replay (Italian), Jennyfer (French), Contigo (Spanish), H&M (Swedish), and Mango (Spanish), not to mention bigger stores like Ikea (Swedish), Metro (German), or Tesco (British). Granted, these are all European chains, and you can add a few American chains like Pizza Hut, Starbucks, and Haagen-Dazs (a particularly odd importation of a pseudo-Scandinavian U.S. brand back to Europe).

Likewise, a report from the New Economics Foundation makes a similar claim, based on a survey of British towns. The report found that—

> 42 of the 103 towns it surveyed in England, Scotland and Wales had become clones, with few local businesses supplied from the surrounding area and a diminished range of specialist outlets. In these towns, independent butchers, greengrocers, pet shops and dry cleaners had been driven out by national supermarket retailers, fast food chains, mobile phone shops and global fashion outlets.[23]

The chains range from national British-only companies to big multinationals like the aforementioned Gap and Starbucks. In many instances, city and town governments actively aided the chains by changing zoning policies to help them dominate the high streets,

The article quotes foundation policy director Andrew Simms as saying,

> Clone stores have a triple whammy on communities. They bleed the local economy of money, destroy the social glue provided by real local shops and steal the identity of our towns and cities. Then we are left with soulless clone towns.... Local people might be excited at first by the arrival of US retailers such as Gap and Starbucks. But they soon tired of "Latte-chino" blandness.[24]

Once the big chains win out, there is no going back to the old town geography. Big chains may lose out, but usually it's to even bigger stores. Undercapitalized shops remain tucked along side streets, if they can persist at all. And as the local merchant class disappears, there is no one left to defend policies of diversification and local ownership.

The future holds a world in which travel will be superfluous, as medieval town squares, tropical beaches, and San Francisco hills only serve as a backdrop for the same world mall in a few flavors with pretty much the same products and the same logos.

TO SUM UP

Standardization is a double-edged sword. Oligopolization, along with mergers and acquisitions, means that some experiences (renting a car, staying in a hotel, having a meal, buying shampoo) are likely to be familiar with no unpleasant surprises and no constant adjustment. But it also means there probably won't be any pleasant surprises either.

The case is that an increasing number of decisions about how your everyday life will look, feel, smell, and taste are being made by fewer and fewer companies, and the people who run those companies think very much alike. But such big companies have become masters at packaging similar experiences in such a way that there seem to be a richness of choices and experiences, all within a safe context.

8 / *Market Domination in Three Industries*

NOW THAT WE'VE ESTABLISHED a wide set of principles in the earlier chapters, let's look at few major concentrated industries in terms of some of the ideas we have discussed. These principles work themselves out in a variety of ways, because every industry has a different history and a different structure. As we've noted before, oligopolies are indeterminate in that they do not follow fixed courses. But they do show different arrangements of the same basic principles.

We will look mostly at the situation in the U.S. market. That market is big, well documented, and coherent—there are none of those major differences in linguistic, economic, or cultural values that make European markets harder to consolidate. The United States, for that reason, is the epicenter of market concentration, though others are rapidly catching up. Mergers and acquisitions are happening everywhere, countries like India and China are starting to invest worldwide, and the same principles now apply to those countries.

The three industries that we will look at (soft drinks, motion pictures, and pharmaceuticals) are worthy of book-length treatments in themselves. All we can do here is suggest some of the workings of increasing oligopolization and market domination. All are concentrating on worldwide markets, although we'll look mostly at U.S. operations, if only because that's where the key companies (with some pharmaceutical exceptions) have their headquarters and biggest operations.

The soft drink industry is an example of the horizontal expansion of a tight, stable oligopoly. The movie industry tries to adapt to changing profit centers and a changing audience by adapting its model of delivery. Finally, the pharmaceuticals industry, a little looser than the others, is in flux, with oligopolies and oligopsonies playing off against each other, as some segments press to disrupt the status quo.

These industries have many more aspects than we can cover here because of their relationship with other industries. For example, in our discussion of pharmaceuticals, there's no room in this volume to discuss managed care companies and other health insurers, hospitals, or even over-the-counter drugs.

All of the concentrated industries here are involved in tiered oligopolies, oligopsonies, and oligonomies (as we discussed in Chapter 2), buying up innovators, influencing government policy, avoiding disruption, creating shifts in the competition matrix, and providing pseudovariety, just to name a few of the points we've discussed already. We'll emphasize the impact of several of these principles for each industry.

THE OLIGOPOLY IN U.S. SOFT DRINKS

One example of a very tight oligopoly is in the U.S. carbonated soft drink market segment. The dominant players in this area (Coca-Cola, PepsiCo, and Cadbury Schweppes) own virtually all of the North American market's most widely distributed and best-known brands. They are dominant in world markets as well, although not all three in every country. These companies' products occupy large portions of any supermarket's shelf space, often covering more territory than real food categories like dairy products, meat, or produce. They take up even more shelf space in convenience stores and local groceries.

As with many mature retail industries, the beverage giants have a problem—growth in the sales of their flagship carbonated products is at a near standstill in the key U.S. market, with 2 percent annual growth or less over the past five years.[1] After years of rapid growth, it seems that the average American can't drink any more flavored, fizzy soda water. To remedy that, these three companies are rapidly expanding both globally, as they expand with existing products, and locally, as they add products from adjacent beverage categories in the supermarket, in categories that are still seeing higher growth.

Cola Wars

The prototype of all marketing and branding struggles is the Cola Wars.[2] PepsiCo and Coca-Cola keep rolling out the big guns: dueling pop stars, and new branded products in the form of "Coca-Cola Blak" and "Pepsi Vanilla," "Coca-Cola Zero" and "Diet Pepsi Jazz." They are fighting on the television, in the fast-food restaurants, and in the supermarkets; they are also dueling in the schools. One of the biggest pushes of the past decades has been convincing school districts, universities, and other institutions to go all-Coke or all-Pepsi, in return for a (small) cut of the gross sales.[3]

Selling costly sugared water and building an increasing demand for it, even in poor countries, involves marketing in its purest form, unsullied by any preexisting need or local tradition. Markets in Eastern Europe, China, India, and Mexico, among others, are expanding faster than U.S. and European markets, and both Coke and Pepsi are securing local partners (bottlers) in these countries to extend their reach. And although the American market may be mature, there's still an opportunity worldwide to replace hot beverages like coffee and tea that require some preparation with these cold, iconic ready-to-drink brands.[4]

All this worldwide activity can't disguise an unpleasant core reality for the vendors: U.S. carbonated soft drink (CSD) sales decreased by 0.7 percent in the year 2005, the first dollar decline in twenty years, after nearly a decade of per capita declines and small absolute gains.[5] That includes declines in both companies' leading brands: at 2 percent lower for Coca-Cola Classic and 3.2 percent for Pepsi. And that's not all. CSD sales in the United Kingdom were down as well,[6] as well as in some other European countries.[7]

Overall U.S. Soda Market

As noted above, Coke and Pepsi have a third major rival on the bottled soft drink shelves, namely Cadbury Schweppes. The Big Three CSD beverage makers now exist in a stable oligopoly that changes only by small increments and which controls around 90 percent of the market. Over the years, Cadbury Schweppes (the result of a merger between a British candy company and a British beverage company) has improved its position by acquiring key (smaller) brands in the United States, namely Dr. Pepper and Seven Up, along with A&W, Sunkist, and Canada Dry. In 2001, it bought moribund Royal Crown Cola so it could compete (just a little) on the cola front.

Although sales are down lately, the carbonated beverage section had been the beneficiary of an amazing record of growth over the past few decades. Consumption has more than doubled over the past 25 years. Americans consumed twice as much soda in 2000 as they did 1980, up from 22 gallons per person per year to more than 56 gallons.[8] Think of that—over a gallon a week for every man, woman, and infant.

In 2000, three companies had almost exactly the same share of the U.S. market as they had in 2004 (see Table 8.1).

Although individual flavors go up and down, the relative market share of the Big Three changes at a glacial rate. The next biggest North American soda company,

Table 8.1 Soft Drink Market Share

Company	Market Share, 2005	Market Share, 2004	Brands
Coca-Cola	43.1%	43.1%	Coke, Sprite, Barq, Fanta, Mello Yello, etc.
PepsiCo	31.4%	31.7%	Pepsi, Mountain Dew, Mug, Slice, etc.
Cadbury Schweppes	14.6%	14.5%	7Up, Dr. Pepper, Schweppes, A&W, Canada Dry, Sunkist, Squirt, etc.

Source: Beverage Digest, March 8, 2005.

Table 8.2 Top U.S. CSD Brands

Rank	Product	Company	Market Share, 2005
1	Coca-Cola Classic	Coca-Cola	17.6%
2	Pepsi-Cola	PepsiCo	11.2%
3	Diet Coke	Coca-Cola	9.7%
4	Mountain Dew	PepsiCo	6.5%
5	Diet Pepsi	PepsiCo	6.0%
6	Sprite	Coca-Cola	5.7%
7	Dr. Pepper	Cadbury Schweppes	5.7%
8	Fanta	Coca-Cola	1.6%
9	Caffeine-Free Diet Coke	Coca-Cola	1.4%
10 (tie)	Sierra Mist and Diet Mountain Dew	PepsiCo	1.4%

Source: Beverage Digest, March 8, 2005.

the Canadian-based Cott Beverage company, has only around 5.4 percent of the market, and that company specializes in supplying private-label soda to supermarkets and other chains. In fact, store-brand soda is the only threat to the Big Three beverage companies, and, so far, it's a manageable one.

Ordinarily, the quickest way to growth in any industry would be through acquisitions. However, the takeover targets in the CSD market that are left are so small that the biggest remaining brand could not make any noticeable difference in total volume for any company.

In spite of the large number of CSD brands and sub-brands (the pseudovariety), there are a limited number of actual products dominating the market, and, while there is some slow movement, these brands aren't going anywhere (see Table 8.2).

In other words, seven products out of the large array of CSD products sold by these companies have nearly 65 percent share of the market, an oligopoly within the oligopoly.

New-Age Beverages

So, how can these companies grow, something we know all oligopolies and all companies are compelled to do? There are two routes the companies have chosen. First, they expand internationally, something the Big Three have been doing for decades, with great success. Second, and even more important for the future, they acquire or add new products in other beverage segments, which show faster growth and less well-defined competition. In fact, other beverage types have, only in the last decade, come into focus as separate, important categories, each with a potential for growth.

So the search for new beverage footholds became the second front of the Cola Wars. And it's surprising how recently this change took place. Most of the acquisitions and new product lines originated in the past decade, as Coca-Cola and PepsiCo until the mid-1990s almost exclusively operated in the carbonated soda segment. There has been a scramble for new territories in beverage shelf space, and all three CSD leaders have invested heavily. These alternative beverage categories were mostly established by start-up or small-cap companies (innovators), including Snapple and Arizona Iced Teas, Odwalla and Nantucket Nectars, and SoBe. The emerging categories began to look like both a threat and an opportunity for the Big Three.

The segments of alternative or new-age beverages ranked by order of sales, are as follows:

- Bottled water (including flavored water)
- Fruit juices and drinks (some shelf-stable, some refrigerated)
- Sports and energy drinks, along with nutrient-enhanced beverages, so called nutriceutical beverages
- Iced tea
- Cold coffee drinks
- Enhanced dairy drinks and soy based "shakes"
- Soy-based and other nondairy beverages[9]

The problem with this market, like most emerging categories in the grocery business, had been an excess of vendors and products, making it hard for retailers to decide who to assign their precious shelf space to. This is accompanied with an even larger number of SKUs of different sizes and flavors, causing general chaos in the market.[10]

The decision for the convenience store and supermarkets comes down, unsurprisingly, in favor of the companies and brands that already dominate the drinks market. As a survey of convenience store chains concluded in 2004, "When selecting a new item for the cold vault, the manufacturer's brand name recognition is the No. 1 element considered."[11]

That made for a great opportunity for the oligopolists, who, while totally absent in the early 1990s, started in the last decade to enter into these markets in a big way. We'll talk about the water category later, but Table 8.3 shows a partial list of the other alternative brands now owned by one of the carbonated Big Three.

Almost all of these products are the result of acquisitions of innovative small companies that established a product profile and proven that there was a market out there. As we have seen in earlier chapters, these innovators end up being the test beds, the skunk works for the big companies. By the time, for example, SoBe had proven that a market existed for its unusual tasting brew, there was no way that the oligopolists were going to let it grow to become a threat.

When the Big Three do buy or (less often) create these products, they already have the salesmen, the vending machines, the bottlers, the money to advertise, and the international reach. They have the deep pockets that allow them to throw a number of products out on the market to see which ones stick.

Table 8.3 Big Three New-Age Beverage Brands

Category	Coca-Cola	PepsiCo	Cadbury Schweppes
Iced tea	Nestea (lic. Nestlé)	Lipton (lic. Unilever), Brisk (lic. Unilever)	Snapple
Sports drinks	Powerade	Gatorade	Mistic
"Health" and energy drinks	Vault, Full Throttle, Tab Extra	SoBe, MDX, AMP, NoFear	Coolah Energy, Solo (Australia)
Coffee and high-caffeine drinks	Planet Java, Coca-Cola Blak	Starbucks (lic.), Pepsi Latte, Frappuccino (lic.), Pepsi X Energy Cola, Pepsi Cino (U.K.)	
Refrigerated juices	Minute Maid, Odwalla	Tropicana, Dole (lic.)	Nantucket Nectars
Shelf-stable juices	Fruitopia	Dole (lic.)	Mauna Lai, Orangina, Mott's, Welch's (lic.), Hawaiian Punch, Clamato
Milk-based drinks	Nestlé Choglit (lic.)	Quaker Milk Chillers	Yoo-hoo, Raging Cow

Source: Company Web sites.
Note: (lic.) denotes a beverage licensed from another company.

They have the ability to crowd rivals off the shelves. With their domination, they have managed to take over a second aisle in many supermarkets and added more refrigerator cases in convenience stores, along with an increase in vending machines. The biggest surprise, however, is in water.

Water Wars

The bottled water industry in North America is growing aggressively. It has been the fastest-growing segment in the beverage industry (around 10 percent annually over the last few years, compared with a decline in carbonated beverages), and the cost of goods sold is almost negligible.[12] Once confined to Perrier and Evian sippers at fancy restaurants or people with bad-tasting local tap water, U.S. consumption has tripled since 1985. As a *Fortune* magazine article put it, "The most brutal battle in the beverage industry is the one for dominance of bottled water. With the niche growing at a 30 percent annual clip, bottled water will likely catapult ahead of coffee and beer to become the second-best-selling beverage—just behind soft drinks—by 2005."[13]

Like other areas of the beverage market, water—once the province of small, local spring bottlers and a few European importers—has now become an oligopoly. Four companies now dominate the North American market for bottled water: Nestlé, Danone, Coca-Cola, and PepsiCo.[14] While Nestlé (originally a Swiss chocolate company) and Danone (originally a French dairy firm) have been in the market for a while, Pepsi and Coke are Johnnies come-lately to the market, PepsiCo in 1995 and Coca-Cola in 1999.

But those two have so much marketing savvy, power in the distribution and bottling area, and store presence, that they have made their two brands, Aquafina (Pepsi) and Dasani (Coke), the top-two selling brands in the U.S. market. That's in spite of the fact that, unlike most of the spring water competitors, these are simply filtered and bottled local tap water. Yet bottles of either of these essentially free liquids sell for almost the same amount as a similar-size container of soda or iced tea. Not a bad business to be in!

Both companies use their vast experience in associating drinks with lifestyle, sharpened during the Cola Wars. They keep ramping up their ad budgets and getting significant growth in volume as they do so.

Nestlé is the overall leader in bottled water, with $3.1 billion in sales and more than 30 percent market share, according in a 2005 survey. The company has a wide variety of brands that are popular in various regions of the country, such as Poland Spring in the east (#3 overall in the United States), Arrowhead and Calistoga in California, Ozarka in the Southwest, and so on. It is also introducing a new global brand, Nestlé Pure Life. These are actual spring waters that have to be trucked to the bottler. Nestlé also sells Perrier, San Pelligrino, and some other European imports.[15]

PepsiCo's Aquafina is the #1-selling water brand in the United States, with over $1.3 billion in yearly sales. Coca-Colas' Dasani is close behind at $1 billion.

Danone, once a major player in the U.S. market (and still a leader world-wide), has retreated, licensing off its interests in local brands like Dannon and Sparkletts, and its global Evian brand, to Coca-Cola. Danone sales were going down even as the water market boomed. (Being #4 can be so hard!)

These four companies have achieved more than 60 percent of the water sales in the United States, and that segment is rapidly expanding. Most other competitors are small and local in scope. (Incidentally, Cadbury Schweppes has a limited water role at present, around 2 percent of the market.)

In the submarket of selling cold individual bottles of water, usually at convenience stores and gas stations, Coca-Cola and PepsiCo are far ahead.[16] This is the high-profit part of the market, more so than in supermarkets, where bulk sales are getting more competitive, as Nestlé, Coke, and Pepsi are starting to compete on price. As a *Wall Street Journal* article noted,

> Coke and Pepsi are trying to avoid a water version of the cola wars, in which they battled it out with price cuts in the supermarket aisle. That's why they're concentrating some 60 percent to 70 percent of their sales in the lucrative business of selling single, cold bottles in convenience stores or vending machines.[17]

But the next step has been differentiating waters by making them vitamin-enriched nutriceuticals or flavored waters. Pepsi, through its Gatorade subsidiary, offers Propel, enhanced with vitamins and minerals and Flavorsplash, flavored water. It is also selling something called Aquafina Essentials, which is flavored water (some sugar added). Coke is selling Dasani Nutriwater, a similar gimmick. Even the water category, only recently discovered by these companies, is now spawning new categories, opening new fronts in the Cola Wars.

To Sum Up

The soft drink beverage industry shows many of the characteristics of oligopoly that we have talked about. Above all, it is a story of horizontal expansion to a neighboring segment, along with international expansion. The same trucks that deliver Coke, Pepsi, and 7Up can deliver Nestea, Aquafina, and Mott's. The territory inside the stores is the same and the buyers know these companies and value their other products, so introducing a new one is welcome. These companies' intense brand management includes a big dose of pseudovariety, as the matrix of flavors and calorie content is worked out.

Like many oligopolies, many of the real innovations have come from smaller companies that have since been bought out and incorporated into the product lines. And the Big Three continually get more like each other as every new product category adopted by one company is quickly adopted by another.

In adopting so fast, these companies have minimized the slowdown and eventual decline in the carbonated beverage market. By buying out the upstarts, they have made for a safe and relatively predictable market with no chance of a disrupting entry from outside. The one big threat is posed by big chains like Wal-Mart and Safeway growing sales of house brands, a trend they spend a lot of marketing dollars to fight.

And like other oligopolies, these companies have been instrumental in creating and dealing with other oligopolies. Only a few companies worldwide produce bottles (Owens-Illinois, Saint Gobain, Anchor Glass) and cans (Crown Holdings, Ball Corporation, U.S. Can, Rexam). A handful of companies (Cargill, Archer Daniels Midland, Staley) supply high-fructose corn syrup. And there are the small number of flavor and fragrances companies (Givaudan, IFF, Firmeniche, Symrise, and Quest International) that essentially make the ingredients that give all commercial beverages their distinctive tastes.

Another layer the big beverage companies have to deal with is their bottlers, who are often independent companies that were given franchises by the companies long ago. The franchises bottle and deliver locally. Coca-Cola especially has been active in repurchasing some of the dealers, to eliminate the middleman, and incorporating them into its subsidiary, Coca-Cola Enterprises.

The next major issue is that the biggest retailers only want to deal with big companies. Wal-Mart is pressuring Coca-Cola to deal with only one company nationally for all deliveries, rather than with many local ones. As of this writing, Coca-Cola Enterprises has started delivering its Powerade beverage nationwide to Wal-Mart warehouses, and Coca-Cola has been sued by a bottlers group of over 60 regional bottlers, saying that doing so breaks a 1994 agreement.[18] Understandably, these bottlers fear that they will be cut out of all sales to major chains.

THE OLIGOPOLY IN THE MOVIE INDUSTRY

The movie industry, as a business, is followed by the general public almost as closely as fans follow the business of professional sports. For years now, the daily newspaper entertainment section has read like *Variety* or *The Hollywood Reporter*, with reports on upcoming projects, financial returns, "bankability" and "Q scores" of various stars, and changes in management at the big studios.

The weekly film grosses stand beside the Major League Baseball standings and the New York Stock Exchange listings as critical numbers to keep tabs on. These haven't overshadowed the usual news of Hollywood divorces, love affairs, and drug busts, but they are taking up a larger part of newspaper gossip columns, television shows (like *Entertainment Tonight*), and magazines (like *Entertainment Weekly*). The plots of the unending supply of chick flicks, gross-out farces, and videogame/comic book–based shoot-'em-ups pale in comparison with the real melodrama, that of the business behind the scenes.

The movie industry is like other oligopolies, in that the pace of change is accelerating. New, often hidden, forces are putting pressure on its every aspect. The existing oligopoly faces a bigger gamble every year. There are several major trends in the industry.

Trend One: Movies Now Have Three Lives—Theater, Video, and Broadcast

The shelf life of movies in theatrical releases is getting shorter and shorter. If you want to see movies at the cineplex, you'd better go there in the first or second week. Unless it's a "blockbuster with legs," it may not be around by the time you have read the reviews, made your decision, and arranged for a babysitter. Even for big hits, any theatrical run of more than six weeks is unusual.

But this short theatrical shelf life is extended by several afterlives, both as videos to rent or buy (once VCR, now DVD), also as TV programs first narrowcast (on pay-per-view, on airplanes, on cable), then broadcast (first on HBO and Cinemax, then on other networks), and, to a growing extent, as downloadables on the Web or on-demand TV. While these aftermarkets were once secondary to the fiscal health of a movie studio, they have become a central part of the finance plans of every film. Because of these aftermarkets, all films have now, in theory, an indefinite shelf life. This factor is changing the way movies are made, distributed, and sold.

Trend Two: International Markets Are as Important as Domestic Markets

Another way of extending shelf life is international release. Increasingly, studios are counting on the U.S. market to simply break even with production costs. They hope to make the real money from the international distribution rights.[19] Global distribution has grown while domestic theatrical releases have plateaued. Enormous Asian markets are just starting to open up. Over the past decade, more and more cineplexes are being built in more and more countries. The international factor was once just icing on the financial cake; now it is fundamental to the planning and making of most Hollywood movies, and some would argue, the "dumbing down" of films for consumption by non-English speakers.[20]

As the U.S. overseas movie market expands, the opposite is not happening. If anything, fewer foreign films are shown in the United States than ever, and even fewer have any serious financial success.

Trend Three: The Blockbuster Mentality Rules

The cost of shelf space in the movie industry is so high that there is little room for modest hits. In our winner-take-all society, you are either a hit or a bomb. Around 500 commercial films are released each year in the United States, 200 of them as major studio releases.[21] The cost of gaining mind space for any one of them is so expensive that smaller films hardly get noticed—and this trend is getting worse. On average, only one new film per week can be a hit each week. That means that 150 of the major studio releases will fall short of hit status.

An average major studio Hollywood film costs $50–75 million to make. It costs $30–50 million to market.[22] Most major studio films that make less than $100 million within a year from release are seen as failures, and that includes most of them. An increasing number of films, like *King Kong* (2005) and *Superman Returns* (2006), have to make nearly $300 million to break even. At that level of risk, though, the payoff can be enormous. The example of monster-hits like *Titanic* (1999) and *The Lord of the Rings* trilogy (2001–2003) wiped out the memory of many expensive bombs.

From a studio's point of view, it's better to swing for the fences than try to get singles and stolen bases, even if you strike out most of the time. The ideal is getting global brand recognition, as the *Matrix* and *Star Wars* franchises do, to drive the aftermarkets. These have a magnifying effect on the few big winners, making them all the more critical to a studio's fortunes. The "can't miss" movie is worth a fortune to the studios—even though it's inevitable that some of them will miss.

Trend Four: Turmoil Rules the Industry—Concentration, Near Bankruptcy, Mergers and Acquisitions

These high stakes, causing the fiscal hysteria of the movie industry, have meant that most companies are a few bombs away from disaster. A few expensive bombs in a row can nearly wipe out a studio. Video distribution firms (the ones that deliver VCRs and DVDs to the retail market) were squeezed out by the studios who brought the job in-house. Video rental stores are almost dead. Six of the top ten movie chains declared bankruptcy in 2000. Studios have merged and been bought out and studio heads keep rolling.

For these reasons, all parts of the industry are tending toward tightly controlled oligopolies run by large international media companies. Their objective is to build a structure that minimizes risk, one that, within the variations in public taste, can help deliver steady profits. Of course, making watchable, innovative films might be a solution, but that's only a minor determinant. The key is to control screens and find ways to gain mind space for a global audience.

The Studio Oligopoly

The top six Hollywood studios control well over 85 percent of the U.S. film industry. All the real independents together have an inconsiderable share of the market, and most of them have to work with or through a major studio to get national distribution.

Of course, oligopoly in the movie industry is nothing new. Up until the 1950s, most of the current motion picture companies were parts of the then-current eight-company "studio system" oligopoly, though relative power and some of the names have changed. In fact, you can argue that in some sense the current oligopoly is less powerful. The 1948 Supreme Court "Paramount Decision" ruled against film industry vertical integration and forced studios to divest themselves of their theaters.[23] The terms have changed somewhat (owning theaters is not all that tempting a risk for most studios), but the oligopoly is pervasive.

But instead of being self-sufficient companies, all of the major studios are now divisions of gigantic international media/industrial empires. Some of them, like Universal Studios, have been bought and sold several times (it's now owned by General Electric/NBC). DreamWorks's independence, guaranteed by the presence of Steven Spielberg, ended in a sale to Paramount (part of CBS and, before a demerger, part of Viacom). MGM/UA, the remnants of two venerable studios that were sucked dry by venture capitalists, was finally sold to Sony and a consortium of other companies, mostly for its fabulous film library. Independents like Miramax and New Line were bought out by the conglomerates years ago. Should one of the independent studios have any real success, it will more than likely be swallowed up as well.

In Table 8.4, the major players in the movie industry are listed by their 2005 ranking, as reported by industry watcher BoxOfficeMojo.[24] In 2005, total U.S. box office sales amounted to $8.8 billion.

The relative rank of the top companies varies from year to year, often depending on one or two blockbusters. Note that these percentages aren't

Table 8.4 The Big Movie Studios

Company	Brands	2005 Gross (millions)	Movies Released	2005 Market Share (includes subsidiaries)
Time Warner	Warner Brothers, New Line, Castle Rock	$1,497	38	20.2%
News Corp	20th Century Fox, Fox Searchlight, TruStar	$1,359	21	15.3%
CBS (formerly Viacom)	Paramount, DreamWorks (acquired in 2006)	$1,334	27	15.1%
Disney	Buena Vista, Miramax, Touchstone, Hollywood, Pixar (acquired in 2006)	$1,104	40	12.5%
Sony	Sony, Columbia, United Artists (acquired in 2005), MGM (acquired in 2005)	$1,000	37	12.5%
Universal	Universal, Focus, Working Title	$1,010	24	11.4%

Source: Based on figures cited at http://www.boxofficemojo.com.

absolute, in that a number of releases are now joint ventures between two or more studios.

Basically, all the major studios offer a new theatrical release every two to three weeks. The films that they deem major get the royal treatment in terms of marketing and distribution. The others get the leavings. Disney and Time Warner issue more films because of their active "independent" subsidiaries, which specialize in smaller, lower-budget, sometimes foreign films.

While the movie-making industry has a looser oligopoly concentration than many others, it is remarkable how convergent the studios are. Executives, stars, writers, and directors jump from one studio to another. The studios sometimes join in backing movies and spreading the financial risk. They all face exactly the same tasks—getting their films produced and then pulling in the audiences. They all work together on the political side, using their trade association, the Motion Picture Association of America (MPAA), to bend government policy and international copyright laws in their favor.

It's no surprise that the people who run the studios share exactly the same culture and the same view of the world. Religious conservatives have been howling about this for years. But it's not some secret, gay, Jewish, liberal conspiracy. More likely, it's just what happens in any oligopoly over time—creeping convergence. It is true that you could reshuffle the management and the scheduled releases of virtually all the major studios and no one would ever notice. Once-unique entities like New Line and Miramax are looking like the studios that absorbed them. And all studios answer to distant CFOs and stockholders who don't care about any ideology except profit.

The Cineplex

A basic problem for studios is how to get their new movies displayed in the right number of theaters across North America to earn maximum profit and prestige. In the 1960s and 1970s, movies were released gradually, with a step-by-step widening of the market as the film built up momentum. Now, the practice is to open big and wide for almost every film. The idea is to grab maximum mind space for the brief moment while the movie is news and the buzz is hot. This game is played out in the interaction between the studios and the national theater chains.

In the last three decades, there has been an explosion of screens in the motion picture industry. Long gone are the days of the stand-alone movie palace. In the 1970s, chains started to build duplex or even four-plex theaters, so movies could share common facilities, including concession stands, parking, and restrooms. The process accelerated in the 1980s, and increasingly bigger theater chains started building multiplexes with eight, ten, even twelve screens, with luxurious stadium seating and a big concession bar (often the only profitable part of the operation), and sometimes even full cafés along with full parking facilities. The AMC theater chain built the first twenty-four-screen megaplex near Dallas in 1994.[25] That set off a building boom, with fourteen plexes and thirty-plexes popping up across the country like mushrooms after a spring shower. Small theater complexes with fewer screens and old seats were out of luck and many closed, just like corner grocery stores or hardware stores.

The leading companies in the business were growing fast, both through acquisitions and upgrading existing theaters. Regional chains were being bought out by fast-moving national chains, and all were adding screens in the suburbs. In 1988, there were around 23,000 screens in the United States. By 2000, there were around 37,000.[26] And most of these were owned by a handful of big national chains.

Oversupply of Screens

By 2000, the chains learned that they'd built too many screens. The industry could not support all these new seats in the same markets. While the number of screens had increased by 50 percent over the period from 1990 to 2000, viewership had gone up only by some 20 percent, a few percent each year.[27]

And although most chains hiked prices (by over 25 percent over the last decade) to help service their debt, there were limits to price hikes, in that there were plenty of other entertainment choices, especially home video. Many people asked themselves why they should go to see a so-so film when it would be available on video in a few months or on TV in half a year. A period of unusually poor (from the box office point of view) movies in the 1999–2000 season didn't help. In 2000 and 2001, a number of chains started declaring bankruptcy. These included Carmike, Loews, United Artists, General Cinema, and Edwards Cinemas, along with several smaller chains. The other chains were all teetering on the brink.

Theater revenues have actually increased in the last two years, thanks to a number of blockbusters and major ticket price increases. But this may be a short-term fix. While the popularity of movies goes up and down, the oversupply of theaters is still a major problem.

One industry analyst calculated that, on the whole, the movie theaters work at 12 percent of capacity or less.[28] In other words, over 80 percent of seats, on average, are empty. That's no surprise when we learn that 80 percent of attendance comes in the three weekend days, meaning that four days a week most theaters are nearly empty, hardly earning enough to pay the electricity to operate the popcorn machine and pay the (minimum) wages of the ticket-takers. Like restaurants, movie theaters make their big money on Fridays, Saturdays, and Sundays.

The oversupply of screens had hurt the industry badly. More than 350 theaters, comprising 1,888 screens, were closed during the year 2000 alone.[29] These closures represented 5 percent of America's theaters and its approximately 39,000 screens. A number of others have closed since then, and the rate of building new ones has slowed considerably. There are now 34,000 to 37,000 screens, but some industry analysts think there are still perhaps 5,000 screens too many for a profitable industry. As we've pointed out, at some point, shelf space becomes a zero-sum game. New theaters simply reshuffle audiences; they don't attract new ones.

Over the past five years, Edwards Theaters, General Cinema, and Universal Studios Theaters were sold to the survivors. Hoyts Cinema, an Australian chain,

Table 8.5 U.S. Theater Chains

Company	Other Theaters Owned	U.S. Theaters (approx.)	U.S. Screens (approx.)
Regal Cinema	United Artists, Hoyts, Edwards	600	6,600
AMC Theaters	General Cinema, Loews Cineplex	415	5,000
Cinemark	Century	399	4,430
Carmike Theaters	Showcase, Multiplex, Cinema	300	2,500
National Amusements	De Lux, The Bridge, IMAX	90	1,200

Source: Company information.

left the U.S. market and sold out to Regal. In 2005, #3 Loews Cineplex sold out to #2 AMC. Century Theaters (then #5) sold out to Cinemark. As shown in Table 8.5, the top-four chains now own over 50 percent of the screens. Not only that, but the Big Four chains own most of the best locations in choice suburban areas and more seats.

These theater chains have developed an oligopsony to counter the movie theater business against the oligopoly of the studios. And they need some power, as running movie chains has been a disastrous business in the last decade.

The bankruptcies that have allowed for further consolidation are due to the twisted economics of the business. In general, some 60 to 70 percent of the first two weeks' box office collections go directly to the studio and distributor. In the third week, the share is 50 percent. The theater owner's percentage goes higher as the movie stays longer, up to 70 percent at week six. However, few films last that long. And, after all, 70 percent of a $2,000 take is not even close to 70 percent of $20,000, which is what the studio can get per screen in the first week of most films.[30]

These agreements make the studio all the more eager to bring in another film to drive in a fresh set of profitable viewers, and the studio is already looking ahead to the video release of the current movie in the first two or three weeks. There is some hope that bigger movie chains will lead to better terms for the studios, though this is slow in coming.[31]

The Real Money

The movies themselves, as it turns out, are "loss leaders" for the theater owners. The theaters have to make their income from the snacks and soft drinks concessions rather than box office take. That's why the prices are so high—and the portions so jumbo—at the snack bar. Popcorn reportedly is 90 percent profit, and soda is marked up by 300 percent or more.[32] It's also why attracting teens has become important to the chains; adults don't spend as much on concessions.[33]

Chains are also making money from selling increasing amounts of advertising in front of their audiences before the film begins. [34] In fact, the three biggest movie chains have a joint venture, National CineMedia, which sells and distributes pre-movie advertising and the preshow "entertainment" bits (previews and entertainment news) that space out the commercials—another case of so-called rivals having totally aligned interests, as friendly enemies.

Pre-movie advertising is booming, with $400 million spent in 2005 and growth of 15 percent per year estimated. It's a new revenue source for the big chains, which have a truly captive audience (no channel surfing, no fast forward), something television advertisers can't offer any more. Plus (for teen-oriented films), the theater chains can deliver an ideal demographic. A 20-minute advertising blitz before the movie has become standard.[35] That added income is starting to make the business of exhibiting films a profitable one again.

In spite of their oligopsony, the big chains have little real leverage with studios in terms of rates (the costs of exhibiting the films). But they do have some power in negotiating which films they will expend their valuable theater space on. Of course, a guaranteed blockbuster will get a showing, perhaps even a few screens in each cineplex. Beyond that, theater operators are interested in films that are relatively short (more turnovers and more advertisements) and that attract popcorn eaters and Coke drinkers. As movie economics expert Edward Jay Epstein puts it, "Will a movie attract enough consumers of buckets of popcorn and soda to justify turning over multiple screens to it?"[36] Next time you complain about the lack of serious, adult-oriented films at your neighborhood theaters, think popcorn.

Movie theater chains are the ultimate in convergence: the movies they show, the decor, the snacks, and now the advertising blitzes are all but identical. The Big Three have sifted out the essential experience and are clearly undifferentiated, joint-venturing "friendly enemies." Their biggest fear is disruption: in part, from a lack of films that attract wide audiences (as happened to some extent in 2005), but longer-term, from the attraction of other media, including motion pictures in other formats.

Movies and Choice

With so many theatrical screens across the country, you'd think you'd have a wide variety of products (films) available at one time. In fact, the opposite has happened. The expansion of the big chains has led to the demise of independent second-run theaters that would prolong a film's life considerably while offering reduced-price tickets and a greater number of currently playing films. In addition, the studios are not interested in the meager revenue from second-run theaters, revenue that would have no impact on later video or television sales. They want to clear the decks for the next release, and move into the aftermarket.

At this point, all the studios and all theater chains have basically the same strategy—show the biggest hits as soon as they are available. If they are megahits, show them on two or more screens in the same cineplex, with staggered starting hours. This strategy will presumably pull in as big an audience as possible as fast as possible.

As we have noted above, the cineplexes are only looking for a narrow range of products, preferably ones that can bring in a quick-decision-making (popcorn-loving) crowd who wants to be in the theater as soon as possible to see the hottest films. This means films that are already presold thanks to: big stars, remakes of famous movies or sequels to other hits, or enormous marketing campaigns designed to bring out the audience. Only a limited number of movies come out with one, two, or especially all three of these factors in their favor. Those are the ones that the theater chains really want. So that's why they all have the same set of 15 to 20 movies, playing in every theater at the same time.

The numbers tell the story. Big studio new releases fill around 3,000 to 3,500 screens apiece; slightly older (three to six weeks after release) or less popular pictures occupy 1,000 or fewer screens each. At any one time, almost half of the national screen capacity is taken up by the top six films and four-fifths of all screen capacity is taken up by 20 to 25 films.[37]

Getting into lots of theaters at first and staying on at the theater for the full six weeks is critical to a movie's financial success and is in no way easy. Once released, the clock is ticking.

The Battle for Mind Space

There's an ultimately even more important reason why studios release their films on as many screens as possible. Generating a high box-office figure functions as a promotion for the film, a way of gaining mind space. In this hall of mirrors, the fact that the marketing effort pulled out large numbers to the opening weekend is seen as a near-guarantee of its "hit" status, thus gaining it mind space for the next few weeks, no matter what the critics say. People want to go to the hot movie, and the movie is hot because other people went to it and talked about it.[38] Thus, a winner-take-all mentality drives the industry. What else could explain the incredible success of such an unlovable movie as 2006's *Pirates of the Caribbean: Dead Men's Chest*, about which one critic notes, "It's hard to shake the feeling that you've been bullied into [going]?"[39]

The buzz carries over from the theatrical release to the TV showings and the DVD release.

To Sum Up

The movie industry is a paradox. The weakest players in the game are the movie chains, an industry dependent on popcorn sales. Yet, that desire to sell more popcorn has a decisive effect throughout the industry. A certain type of movie keeps the theater chains happy, and the need to attract the right kind of audience drives their actions, and eventually the actions of the studios.

Movies have to do well in their short time-window in the theaters. That popularity cascades through the system, with a direct impact on DVD sales and broadcast rights, not to mention licensing fees and other side sources of income.

In a way, the big studios, as seemingly powerful as they are, have their hands tied by the need to keep the theater chains filled. The result is a distinct lack of interest in films that appeal to people over 20. As one multiplex owner told a studio executive, "The less dialogue the better. The teens that come to our theaters want car chases, bombs, a few beautiful bodies, and mind-bending special effects."[40] The discipline of the market, in this case, has constrained the behavior of the oligopoly. That oligopoly is a very well-off cog in a machine that it has little control over.

THE OLIGOPOLY IN THE PHARMACEUTICAL INDUSTRY

The world health care industry has had over 10,000 mergers and acquisitions since 1993, almost 1,000 a year. These deals in managed care, drug companies, biotech companies, device manufacturers, insurers, and all the companies that support them have resulted in an ever-increasing industry consolidation.[41]

The numbers are staggering: an average of nearly 1,000 mergers and acquisitions a year, that's almost three each day. And many of the deals tracked are for hundreds of millions of dollars, even billions. It stands as testimony to the speedy consolidation of the health care marketplace, a concentration that seems to be continuing apace. This reshaping of one of America's most profitable industries takes place with little public notice, even though availability of health care and drugs is among the biggest political issues of our time.

We'll discuss concentration in the drug industry, itself a vast topic we can only sketch in here. Basically, we see concentration going on in five distinct areas:

- The prescription drug market led by companies like Pfizer and Merck
- The growing generic drug market led by less-well known companies like Teva and Sandoz
- The over-the-counter segment, which includes drugs and health equipment
- The pharmacy benefit manager who helps insurance companies decide on which drugs will be ordered
- The drugstore chains

Big Pharma

While it's not a tight oligopoly like the soft drink industry, the U.S. prescription pharmaceutical industry has been rapidly consolidating over the past few decades. The $60 billion Pfizer-Pharmacia merger in 2000 was the biggest move in a trend that saw the ingestion of such venerable companies as Upjohn, Burroughs Wellcome, Parke-Davis, and Warner-Lambert. What were several dozen large companies in the 1980s were consolidated into a dozen major global pharmaceutical companies.

You can see that trend even in the compound names of a company like GlaxoSmithKline, which represents the cumulative consolidation of half a dozen companies that a little more than a decade ago were all separate. You can also see it in company names like Novartis and Sanofi-Aventis, which are just made-up futuristic names invented at the merger of older, familiar companies. Novartis is the result of the 1996 merger of Swiss companies Ciba-Geigy and Sandoz Laboratories; Sanofi-Aventis is the result of the 1999 merger of French Rhone-Poulenc and German-based Hoechst, followed by the 2004 merger of Aventis with Sanofi Synthélabo, itself the result of a 1999 merger between two French companies (boxes within boxes!).

Why so many mergers and acquisitions? There are the many economic reasons we've discussed in earlier chapters, of course, and the rush for expansion to keep investors happy. Aside from that, a big reason is a desire to influence the many public policy decisions that affect the industry. Pharmaceutical companies are involved more than ever in politics, from drug pricing policies to such issues as patent enforcement, drug testing, lawsuit liability, imported drugs, subsidized bird flu vaccines, and African AIDS relief. It stands to reason that larger companies can swing more political heft and have an influence on government health policies. In addition, the massive sales, advertising, research, and testing costs require companies with deep pockets, with lobbying bills in the hundreds of millions.[42]

Total U.S. prescription drugs sales were around $235 billion in 2004, including patent and generic (off-patent) drugs. It can be argued that a group with ten to fifteen members, the largest of which has a 13.5 percent market share, and for which the top-four companies control only around 34 percent of the market is not much of an oligopoly. And even those market leaders are in a precarious position, particularly because some key patents run out this decade, including many of those listed in Table 8.6.

The Statin Oligopoly

But a lot depends on how you look at the market and on how you divide the market into segments. Consolidation is much greater in specific therapeutic areas. The leading drug category in terms of sales is statins, cholesterol lowering drugs such as Lipitor (Pfizer), Zocor (Merck & Company), Lescol (Novartis), Crestor (AstraZeneca), and Pravachol (Bristol-Myers Squibb).

These are important drugs in terms of pharmaceutical company revenues, because they are used by a remarkably high and growing percentage of the population and because they are lifetime drugs requiring daily use. It costs over $100 a month (whether the user or his health insurance pays) to use such drugs.[43]

Sales of statins grew by 12 percent in 2004. In that significant submarket ($15 billion), Pfizer's Lipitor had 50 percent of the market in 2004. In that category, Merck's Zocor had around 30 percent. (In fact, these two drugs were the #1- and #2-selling drugs for any condition.) In one critical industry segment, two companies had 80 percent of the market. In 2004, Merck introduced

Table 8.6 Top-Ten U.S. Pharmaceutical Companies

Rank	Company	2004 U.S. Prescription Sales (billions)	Market Share	Merged Entities (sample)	Drugs (sample)
1	Pfizer	$30.7	13.1%	Warner-Lambert, Pharmacia, Parke-Davis, Searle, Upjohn	Lipitor, Viagra, Xanax, Zoloft
2	GlaxoSmithKline	$18.7	8%	Burroughs Wellcome, Smith, Kline, French, Beckman, Norcliff Thayer, Beecham, Sterling	Amoxil. Compazine, Paxil, Serevent, Thorazine, WellButrin
3	Johnson & Johnson	$16.2	6.9%	Roc, MacNeil, Janssen	Novum, Ortho, Procrit, Remicade, Risperdal
4	Merck	$15.0	6.0%	Merck Sharp & Dohme	Crixivan, Invanz, Propecia, Zocor
5	AstraZeneca	$11.3	4.8%	Astral, ICI/Zeneca, Stuart	Accolate, Diprovan, Nexium, Prilosec, Zoladex
6	Novartis	$10.2	4.2%	Sandoz, Ciba-Geigy	Cinacen, Diovan, Larrasil, Lescol, Lotrel
7	Sanofi-Aventis	$10.3	4.3%	Rhone-Poulenc, Hoechst, Connaught Labs, Merieux	Actonel, Allegra, Arava, Ketek, Lantus
8	Amgen	$9.5	4.1%	—	Epogen, Enbrel, Kineret
9	Bristol-Myers Squibb	$9.2	3.9%	Mead Johnson, DuPont Pharmaceuticals	Avapro, Glucovance, Prevachol, Taxol, Tequin
10	Wyeth	$8.2	3.4%	American Home Products, Ayerst, Lederle	Alesse, Efflexor, Norplant, Premarin, Sonata

Source: Based on figures cited at http://www.imshealth.com.

a new statin drug, with the brand name Vytorin, which by 2005 had over 10 percent of the market share and climbing.[44] That's just in time, as Merck loses its Zocor patent in 2006 and is likely to see new competition.

This statin oligopoly has real power. Although a generic drug solution (Lovastatin, also known as Mevacor or Altocor) is efficacious, it is nowhere near as widely prescribed as the patented drugs. *Consumer Reports* estimates that U.S. taxpayers alone could save over $8 billion if suitable generic drugs were used in place of the leading patented drugs.[45] Pfizer and Merck have managed to dominate the market through an energetic marketing campaign and a nonstop sales effort directed at physicians.[46] At the same time, Pfizer managed to raise prices for Lipitor by 5.8 percent in 2005.

Drug Company Specialization

That is the most extreme case in terms of dollars, but most drug companies, once complete generalists, now stake out their territory by dominating more specific submarkets—in vaccines, in cancer drugs, in diabetes, in antidepressives, and so on. The trend of the last five years has been to concentrate on about half a dozen specialty disease categories, not to take a scattershot approach, and as a result companies have sold off (discarded) some product lines (even divisions) and picked up others.

For example, Pfizer bought and entered into joint ventures with several companies developing ophthalmic drugs for treating conditions like macular degeneration and glaucoma. Sanofi-Aventis decided in 2004 to specialize in four areas: (1) oncology; (2) diabetes; (3) respiratory, central nervous system, and cardiovascular diseases; and (4) vaccines.[47] Bristol-Myers Squibb, according to its Web site, is focused on "Alzheimer's disease, atherosclerosis, diabetes, hepatitis, HIV/AIDS, obesity, and rheumatoid arthritis."[48] Other big companies have similar focuses.

Meanwhile, most have deliberately shaved off noncore businesses. Novartis spun off its agrochemical business in 1999 as Syngenta, sold much of its food business off in 2002, and divested its health and nutrition business in 2005. Aventis in 2003 sold its specialty chemicals business and also its blood products division. GlaxoSmithKline in 2006 sold its animal health division.

There are many other, smaller pharmaceutical and biotech research firms, but more and more these companies exist by forming alliances for distribution and marketing with the big companies. They are slowly becoming research satellites of the biggest drug companies. Merck has licensed over 100 drugs from biotech firms over the past five years,[49] as the drug giants pour R&D dollars into start-ups and turn themselves into middlemen.[50]

Such joint ventures are needed to keep the drug pipeline flowing. As we have noted in earlier chapters, the lack of innovation is catching up to the biggest companies. Merck, Glaxo, and Pfizer are especially in peril due to the end of the line for some top sellers. And the pipelines have not been replenished, at least not with comparable high-use drugs. [51] But one area is catching fire: the generic drugs business, a sector that is not dependent on its own innovations.

More Consolidation in Generic Drugs

The 1990s saw major mergers and acquisitions in the patent pharmacy industry, as companies like Aventis and Novartis were created and other major players were bought out. In the 2000s, the major merger and acquisition activity has shifted to the generic sector. The generic drug market, which sells prescription drugs past their patent, is growing rapidly—faster than the overall pharmaceutical industry. And that growth is especially strong in total numbers of prescriptions, as prices are lower and margins thinner with generics.[52]

In 2004, the world market for generic drugs was almost $40 billion, and it is estimated that it will rise to over $80 billion by the end of the decade.[53] U.S. generic sales are up as well: over $27 million in 2005, accounting for over 10 percent of all drug sales by dollars, a figure over 60 percent higher than originally predicted.[54] Over 50 percent of prescriptions being filled in the United States are generics, up from 19 percent in 1984, though they are, of course, far less profitable than prescription drugs. Furthermore, around three dozen major medicines, including many of the best sellers, have recently lost or are due to lose patented status over the next few years.

As the generic drug industry gets more prominent, there's been a continual parade of acquisitions consolidation in that market as well.[55] In the area of nonbranded generics, the top four vendors in the sector have 55 percent of the U.S. market, a serious oligopoly (see Table 8.7). Industry leader Teva fills one of every sixteen prescriptions in the United States.[56]

Note that Sanofi is #2 worldwide and was #1 until Teva's latest acquisitions. Over the past few years, the mergers and acquisitions have been fast and furious. And among the top companies, they have been especially rapid.

Recent Major Generic Drug Consolidation Deals

Here is a sample of the recent generic drug consolidation deals:

- 2003 Sandoz (Novartis) bought Slovakia's Lek for $800 million.
- 2004 Israeli firm Teva acquired U.S.-based Sicor.

Table 8.7 U.S. Generic Prescription Drug Leaders, 2004

Rank	Corporation	Market Share
1	Teva	13.2%
2	Mylan	12.6%
3	Watson	9.2%
4	Sanofi	8.3%
5	Ivax	5.2%

Source: Based on figures cited at http://www.imshealth.com.

- Teva bought Italy-based Dorom from Pfizer for $885 million.
- Sandoz (Novartis) acquired Canada's Sabex for more than $500 million and Denmark's Durascan from AstraZeneca (for an undisclosed sum).
- 2005 Novartis acquired German-based Hexal and U.S.-based Eon Labs in a connected deal for $8.3 billion.
- Teva acquired U.S.-based Ivax (#5 on our list) for $7.4 billion.
- 2006 Watson Pharmaceuticals Inc. bought U.S. rival Andrx for $1.9 billion.
- Mylan acquired controlling stake in Indian drugmaker Matrix ($730 million).

Aside from these, scores of other deals have taken place between lower-ranking companies, and the consensus is that there are many more in the planning stages.[57]

Consolidation is rife in the generics industry, because the key companies look for global scale, and there is a feeding frenzy in the works as the big companies seek to build competitive position. With profits per sale so much smaller than those of the patented pharmaceutical companies, generics companies desire to sell the widest set of drugs possible. Scale has become the overriding factor.

It is interesting that over the years most of the big patent pharmaceutical companies have sold off their generic drug operations (Novartis is the big exception). Pfizer sold its generic operations to Merck KGaA (the German drug company, not to be confused with the U.S.-based Merck & Company) in 2004.[58] The reason would seem to be the difficulty of owning competing businesses under the same roof. It's hard to compete against yourself, with two such different profit models.

The truth is that Big Pharma is no longer fighting against small local, nameless generic companies. The existence of a multinational oligopoly in patent drugs has given rise to a multinational oligopoly in generic drugs (in this case, oligopoly generates oligopoly). Generic companies are girding up for the fight to supply patients and insurance companies. Big Pharma is now competing with Big Generics.[59] Above all, Big Pharma and Big Generics are trying to get the attention of a powerful oligopsony that acts as gatekeeper to the end user.

Pharmacy Benefit Managers

If you have health insurance in the United States, you have probably run into the following problem: your doctor prescribes a drug, but your insurance company tells you it won't pay for it. You can, however, receive another drug that is judged to have similar properties. Sometimes the drug is a generic; sometimes it is just a different patented medicine from another major drug company. What drugs are accepted by your insurer is determined by what is called a *formulary*; in this case, the original drug was not included in the formulary.

In general, these formularies are determined by a set of companies called Pharmacy Benefit Managers (PBMs). These companies act as middlemen between drug companies on the one side and insurance companies, pharmacies, hospitals, government health plans, and managed care plans on the other. They evaluate the effectiveness of drugs and create formularies of the most cost-effective drugs for treating each condition or disease. And they bargain to get the lowest price from the drug companies.

Currently, there are over 50 PBMs. But, in reality, just three major companies have a large majority of the market. These companies are:

- Medco Health Solutions, the largest PBM, with 2005 income of $37 billion and 65 million members
- Caremark Rx, with $32 billion in sales and 90 million members
- Express Scripts, with $16 billion in sales and 50 million members

With over 200 million participants (some in Canada), these companies control over two-thirds of the PBM market. That means they control vast amounts of prescriptions. Medco, for example, handles 550 million prescriptions each year.

This industry has a long history of mergers. In fact, Caremark merged with AdvancePCS in 2003 (combining the #3 and #4 PBMs); AdvancePCS itself is the result of a 2000 merger between Advanced Paradigm and PCS Health Systems. In the early 1990s there were many small and midsize PBMs. But then the big drug companies started acquiring them and rolling them up. In the end, under the threat of antitrust lawsuits, they had to spin them off or sell them. Merck, for example, spun off Medco in 2002.

The big temptation in PBMs' gatekeeper role, of course, is kickbacks. Just as radio stations have been in a position to attract payola from record companies, so did PBMs attract money from the drugmakers. There's so much money to be earned here that the situation naturally breeds dubious practices. With even fewer players, the temptation (and the rewards) will be even greater. Indeed, Medco just paid a $155 million fine for kickbacks from drug companies.[60]

Aside from regulating which drugs get accepted by which insurance programs, PBMs also have become major providers of prescription drugs to patients through mail order. Medco's mail-order business generated over $14 billion net in 2005, and there are similar operations at the other two companies.[61]

This move into the mail-order business has made the PBMs direct competitors of the major drug chains—a major shift in the competition matrix, as pharmacies start to compete with a new threat.

U.S. Drugstore Chains

The big drugstore chains in the United States are basically down to three. These chains have enormous advantages over mom-and-pop pharmacies and even over smaller chains. They can offer longer opening hours and ample parking, making them more convenient for shoppers. They allow shoppers to combine several shopping tasks at once (groceries, birthday cards, alarm clocks,

Table 8.8 Major U.S. Drugstore Chains

Company	Stores (approx.)	Annual Sales (billions)
Walgreens	5,400	$42
CVS	6,200	$37
Rite Aid	3,300	$17

Source: Company information.

shampoo) while waiting for their prescription to be filled. They can stock a larger inventory of drugs, so they can easily meet most demands.

But most of all, they have the advantages of an oligopsony. They can negotiate face to face with the big drug manufacturers and other suppliers to get the best discounts. They can assert pressure over the major health insurance companies in terms of discounts and speed of reimbursement. They can work with the PBM oligopoly to maintain their margins. That's all on top of efficiencies in administration, accounting, and distribution (see Table 8.8).

This oligopoly became even tighter over the past few years by the partition of the #4 chain Eckerd to CVS and Canadian chain Jean Coutu in 2004. Rite Aid bought Jean Coutu's U.S. stores in 2006. Supermarket chain Albertson's breakup led to 700 drugstores (mostly Osco) going to CVS in 2005.

Drug Disruption

Having put thousands of small local drugstores and chains out of business, the big drug chains were ready to claim a comfortable oligopoly position. But they were hit by a shift in the competition matrix. First, the PBM mail-order business ate into traffic.

After a long refusal to deal with a changed world, the Big Three drugstore chains have set up their own mail-order divisions. Walgreens and CVS have also started offering 90-day prescriptions in the store through their own PBM divisions (after getting insurance companies to change their rules).[62] Nothing really kept drugstores from doing so previously; nothing, that is, except their desire to see customers coming back for refills every month.[63] The drugstores are fighting back with this new service.

Then the big disruptor came knocking—Wal-Mart, whose offer to sell generics at very low cost has sent a chill through the drugstore chains and the PBMs alike. Indeed, the Wal-Mart announcement that it would sell a large number of generic drugs for $4 apiece has the potential to restructure the market for everyone in the drug industry—parent drug companies, generics makers, PBMs, and drugstore chains.

The race toward generics is likely to accelerate, and the price structure that patent drug companies have depended on for years is under threat. As more and more of the most commonly used drugs have generic forms and only intense marketing campaigns can get such narrowly focused drugs a big buy-through, it's hard not to see a slippery slope, even an avalanche, in drug prices. Wal-Mart's move may be the biggest innovation in health care in the decade, the creative destruction that rearranges the whole industry.

As one observer of the market put it,

> The fundamental problem facing chain drugstores is that if the likes of Walgreens, CVS, and Rite Aid match Wal-Mart's prices on generic prescription drugs, the group will be slashing profits on one of its most lucrative products. Yet any customer who no longer goes to the local drugstore to pick up a prescription each month because the prices are higher is also a customer who will no longer be buying magazines, drinks, groceries, or other products there. Drugstores, in fact, may face a situation similar to music stores' conundrum years ago, when Best Buy began selling CDs cheaply to drive customers to its stores.[64]

One sudden twist, just announced as we went to press, was the attempted acquisition of Caremark by CVS, a move by the #2 drugstore chain to buy the #2 PBM. This looks like a move that might shift the competition matrix once again. The competition between the PBM layer and the drugstore chain layer may be eliminated again.

To Sum Up

The drug industry is a tiered oligonomy, with intense oligopoly/oligopsony struggle between increasingly big forces. Two other tiers we can't pursue here, due to space limitations: the health insurance and managed care companies that hire the PBMs to act for them, and the hospital groups and medical practices (constantly getting larger) that prescribe the drugs.

The competition matrix keeps evolving, as the Wal-Mart example shows. There's also the factor of slowest innovation at the biggest companies, who are desperately trying to extend their patents through legal and regulatory means and buy up the small innovative firms that are developing drugs.

CONCLUSION

Although concentration and oligopolization are features of essentially all industries, each has its own history, its own pattern of innovation and disruption, and its own layers of buyers and sellers, and each has developed in its own way. The principles are common, but the effect of those principles is varied.

Fundamentally, all layers of these and other industries are seeking to narrow choice, whether that of consumers or suppliers, while (at least to consumers) giving the illusion of constant variety. All are involved in influencing government policy in a serious way, in many cases involving the protection of intellectual property. All are limited by various factors in their ability to raise prices but have found other ways to increase revenues. All are far more concentrated than they were a few years ago. All three of these industries are in relatively mature markets, so squeezing out new growth requires constant activity and endless adjustments in terms of acquisitions and de-acquisitions, reshuffling of personnel, and refreshing the product line.

Furthermore, all companies at all layers constantly feel themselves under attack and see themselves as persecuted. The soft drink companies fight against dietary panels that discourage the excess use of their products. The motion picture industry fights against piracy. The pharmaceutical business has a host of enemies, ranging from trial lawyers to insurance companies. A strong sense of paranoia leads to strategies of aggressive defense. After all, all three industries have to deal with the retailing juggernaut Wal-Mart and its imitators.

Conclusion

TWO OPPOSED MORAL ABSOLUTES

A THOUGHT-PROVOKING POST on a Web site called Antitrust Review considers the question of moral disapproval and antitrust policy and, by extension, applies this question to the oligopolies that are the subject of this book.[1] The debate about more or less regulatory control over business is not so much an argument about economic theories, that is, free market versus populism, but rather it is moral issues divide the two positions.

The article quotes a paper by William H. Page, a law professor and antitrust expert at the University of Florida, who presents two basic ideologies in the debate. One sees the market as an "evolutionary" and ultimately self-correcting means for exchange; the other, what he calls the "intentional vision," sees the market as

> a mechanism within which powerful interests can coerce consumers, labor, and small businesses; market structures, consequently, tend toward monopoly. In the intentional vision, the unfair outcomes of market processes can and should be corrected by democratic, governmental intervention, including direct regulation.[2]

Hanno Kaiser at Antitrust Review takes this perceptive dichotomy one step further and talks about two moral positions. One he calls "wealth as a sign of moral goodness," which holds that "in a free market economy, one can only get rich by serving others."

The other moral stance sees "wealth as a sign of moral corruption" As Kaiser writes, "Free, consensual exchanges" only exist among equals in power. In every other case, "the strong do what they can and the weak suffer what they must. The implication is that one can get rich only by exploiting others."[3]

These visions of the world, he argues, animate "much of the discussion about free markets, regulation, big business, socialism, distributive justice, and globalization." Both views, he argues, "are idealisms, reflective more of individual value commitments than of how the world really works."

The evolutionary standpoint is the orthodoxy of the right (whoever wins the race is right), while the left is tied to a sense that whoever wins the race is, by definition, a cheater or a criminal. The world seems now divided between those who want to roll back the regulation of business completely (The Club for Growth) and those who want to crush big companies or, at least, regulate their every transaction (People's Global Action).

In this book, we have tried to assume that free markets are imperfect, but they provide many benefits, and that corporations are not innately evil, but they are capable of destructive acts. The heads of corporations are under enormous pressures and have enormous temptations. Serious regulation, starting with antitrust and antifraud protection, is needed to maintain free markets, and the penalties for seriously illegal and anticompetitive acts should be serious in turn.

The biggest danger, as I see it, is the effect of money on politics. It is one thing to have a disagreement about how much an industry should or should not be regulated, but when the leaders in an industry have bought a seat at the decision-making table, and had their own lawyers actually write up the government regulations, there is no more thought of a philosophical discussion. Similarly, when tax accountants, government buyers, environment regulation monitors, and antitrust lawyers are discouraged from doing their jobs in order to reward companies supporting the government, then the situation is bad indeed.

The argument about whether or not free markets are good is rendered moot when the market is not really free. Our position (echoing Gandhi on Western civilization) on the question of what we think of free markets is that "We think it would be a good idea."

WHAT WOULD ADAM SMITH SAY?

Adam Smith, the eighteenth-century intellectual godfather of free-market capitalism, in his book *The Wealth of Nations* made the seminal defense of the free market. He saw that the self-interests of the investor/proprietor were fully compatible with, even the cause of, the public good. He is the patron saint of laissez-faire.

Self-interest is built into Smith's theories, and he has no illusions about the motivating role selfishness has in keeping the economy rolling. As he famously wrote, "It is not from the benevolence of the butcher, the brewer, or the baker, that we can expect our dinner, but from their regard to their own interest." Perhaps he'd write today of the interest of Tyson, Anheuser-Busch, and Nabisco/Kraft/Altria, our modern-day butcher, brewer, and baker.

But even Smith foresaw the perils of excessive concentration in business. He understood that this state of benevolent general good was dependent on competition and that most of the investor/proprietors were anything but benevolent about competition. As Smith states in Chapter 9 of *The Wealth of Nations*:

The interest of the dealers [stockholding class], however, in any particular branch of trade or manufactures, is always in some respects different from, and even opposite to, that of the public. To widen the market and to narrow the competition, is always the interest of the dealers. To widen the market may frequently be agreeable enough to the interest of the public; but to narrow the competition must always be against it, and can serve only to enable the dealers, by raising their profits above what they naturally would be, to levy, for their own benefit, an *absurd tax* upon the rest of their fellow-citizens. (emphasis added)

In other words, the "Invisible Hand" that guides the economy was always in danger of being replaced with a malevolent hand with its fingers ready to tip the scale of commerce. The "absurd tax" is not so much, I have argued, in prices, but rather in costs—costs to employees, small businesses, and farmers; the cost of subsidies; and, ultimately, costs to democracy and society.

Going on, Smith urged legislators to consider carefully any change in laws forced on them by the class of stock owners and dealers, especially when those laws would tend to restrict competition.

The proposal of any new law or regulation of commerce which comes from this order ought always to be listened to with great precaution, and ought never to be adopted till after having been long and carefully examined, not only with the most scrupulous, but with the most suspicious attention. It comes from an order of men whose interest is never exactly the same with that of the public, who have generally an interest to deceive and even to oppress the public, and who accordingly have, upon many occasions, both deceived and oppressed it.

Smith had it right. Unlike some of his present-day disciples, he was well aware of the dangers of someone compromising the system. And he lived a century before the rise of big corporations that put unprecedented power into the hands of a few companies. Smith did not blandly approve of anything that big companies do, and the big companies of his days would look like mom-and-pop operations by today's standards. As Smith points out, what makes individuals rich is not the same as what makes a nation rich. Look no further than Nigeria or Saudi Arabia for examples.

Furthermore, Smith hit the target with his fear of the legislative process being dictated by powerful companies. Governments have ever been eager to interfere in the market, rather than to play the just mediator. From awarding monopolies to court favorites, to doling out no-bid contracts, from regulating health and safety standards to setting trade policy, the government has always been intertwined with business, and those who get to influence government policies and actions often have, as Smith writes, an "an interest to deceive and even to oppress the public."

In the ideal free-market economy of our politicians, every product, even every company, has an equal chance to make it big. But in the real world, entrenched forces combat equal opportunity. The market in most sectors is not a democracy at all. Even the Internet, which was supposed to "change all that" is in danger of becoming still another tool that mostly enhances the power of the big companies that rule major markets.

GLOBALISM AND ITS DISCONTENTS

The internationalization of world commerce is a companion to the growth of megacorporations. Each feeds on the other: big companies push governments to lower trade barriers and allow for foreign ownership, while increased free trade encourages big corporations to get ever bigger, or face losing out to even more massive rivals.

While the breaking down of trade barriers has been an ongoing process since World War II, the steady globalism of the economy was accelerated by the 1995 establishment of the World Trade Organization (WTO), a body charged with the task of getting rid of trade barriers and given the power to settle trade disputes between countries. One result of the establishment of that group has been the immediate increase in transborder mergers and acquisitions and an immediate lessening of national economic independence.

Antiglobalism is a strange movement, if it can be called one. It includes a large cross section of social critics, including reformists, nationalists, socialists, xenophobes, antimodernists, and anarchists. The agendas under its umbrella include advocates for the environment, unions, local companies, and good nutrition, to name but a few. But whatever the starting point, the general perception is that big companies are getting away with evil and that governments need to be pressured to stop them. But, most antiglobalists argue, big government (including international organizations like the World Bank, the International Monetary Fund, and the WTO) is hand-in-glove with the big corporations (Nestlé, Monsanto, and BP).

Most antiglobalist criticisms are based on real problems, especially if we filter out the most fanatical fringe demands. On the other hand, the analysis of the situation is often weak. For many of globalism's critics, real problems are turned into melodramatic struggles of good versus evil. While real conspiracies occur and some individuals are crooks, the economic realities are more complicated than any individual crime or injustice. Along with Smith's invisible hand that delivers the benefits of free markets (and those benefits are real—starting with food, housing, and comfort for most but by no means all), there is a second force, one hurtful to the common good, a force that, taking advantage of the free market, corrodes the economy, government, and society.

That corrosion is not an aberration. It's an outgrowth of the beneficial part of the free market. The government has to be pressured to, as much a possible, keep that force in check. But in an age of mammoth corporations with open purses and access to media and lawyers, and the ability to punish and reward liberally, it will take a concerted effort to keep them in check. The regulation of market dominant companies will need more of that "most scrupulous ... most suspicious attention" Smith asks for.

Notes

INTRODUCTION

1. William G. Shepherd and Joanna M. Shepherd, *The Economics of Industrial Organization*, 5th ed. (Waveland Press, 2004), 227.
2. Ibid., 228.
3. Paul Krugman and Robin Wells, *Microeconomics* (Worth Publishers, 2005), 365.

CHAPTER 1. THE NEW OLIGOPOLY

1. For information on the European Union's continuing antitrust war with Microsoft, look at Joris Evans, "Vista's European Battleground," CNET News, September 18, 2006.
2. Joseph E. Stiglitz and Carl E. Walsh, *Economics*, 4th ed. (W. W. Norton, 2005), 224.
3. Naomi Lamoreaux, *The Great Merger Movement in American Business, 1805–1904* (Cambridge University Press, 1985).
4. For example, Steve Rosenbush, "Investment Banks Jockey for Position," *BusinessWeek*, June 30, 2006; Shaheen Pasha, "Outlook Rosy for 2006 M&A Activity," CNNMoney.com, December 10, 2005; Dennis K. Berman, "Merger Activity Sets Stage for Record Year," *Wall Street Journal*, October 2, 2006.
5. Bank of America, "How Strategic Buyers are Competing in a Changing M&A Market," *Capital Eyes* newsletter, September–October 2006.
6. IAC has since spun off its online travel businesses under the name Expedia.
7. Tony Jackson, "Shades of Old Conglomerates in Private Equity Trend," *Financial Times*, October 31, 2006. Also see Paul O'Keeffe, "The Rise of the New Conglomerates," www.bbcnews.com, February 10, 2005.
8. Available at www.census.gov/epcd/www/concentration.html.
9. Federal Trade Commission, "Cytec Industries, Inc.," Docket no. C-4132. Available at www.ftc.gov.
10. A thorough discussion of this issue is found in a paper by Jonathan B. Baker, "Market Definition," August 2006.

11. "The Little Picture," *Forbes*, March 29, 2004.

12. As noted, among other books, Jack Welch, *Jack: Straight from the Gut* (Warner Business Books, 2001).

13. "A Peep into Jack's Secrets," www.biznet.com, September 22, 2002.

14. As quoted in Robert Slater, *Jack Welch and the GE Way* (McGraw Hill, 1999) and a number of other sources.

CHAPTER 2. OLIGOPOLIES AND OLIGOPSONIES

1. As dramatized in Frank Norris's novel *The Octopus* (1901).

2. "How Rising Wages Are Changing The Game In China," *BusinessWeek*, March 27, 2006.

3. Barry T. Hirsch and Edward J. Schumacher, "Monopsony Power and Relative Wages in the Labor Market for Nurses." *Journal of Health Economics* 14(4):443–76, October 1995.

4. Discussed in William M. Boal and Michael R. Ransom, "Monopsony in American Labor Markets," *Online Encyclopedia of Economic History* (January 2002).

5. Roger Abrams, *The Money Pitch: Baseball Free Agency and Salary Arbitration* (Temple University Press, 2000), as quoted in Marc Edelman, "Has Collusion Returned to Baseball?" *Entertainment Law Review* 24, 2004.

6. Jewel Gopmani, "Airline Woes," *Detroit Free Press*, March 4, 2006.

7. Paul Collins, "Do Bookstores Have a Future?" *Village Voice*, May 22, 2006.

8. Ibid.

9. Chris Anderson, *The Long Tail* (Hyperion, 2006).

10. John Cassidy, "Going Long," *New Yorker*, July 10, 2006.

11. John R. Wilke, "Bully Buyers: How Driving Prices Lower Can Violate Antitrust Statutes," *Wall Street Journal*, January 27, 2004.

12. Unfortunately, the article's subtitle "'Monopsony' Suits Mount As Companies Are Accused of Squeezing Suppliers" confuses monopsonies with oligopsonies. This is an important distinction because it's precisely because there is some competition that these situations traditionally are ignored by antitrust regulators. Also, the problem is not in reducing prices, in general, a good thing, but in reducing costs unfairly.

13. Ibid.

14. Charles Fishman, "The Wal-Mart You Don't Know," *Fast Company*, December 2003.

15. As argued in a report from the McKinsey & Company study, as reported by Virginia Postrel, "Lessons in Keeping Business Humming, Courtesy of Wal-Mart," *The New York Times*, February 28, 2002.

16. Steven Greenhouse, "Wal-Mart, Driving Workers and Supermarkets Crazy," *New York Times*, October 19, 2003.

17. Charles Fishman, *The Wal-Mart Effect* (Penguin Press, 2006), 163.

18. "China's Steelmakers Hold Out As Suppliers Set Pricing Deals," *Wall Street Journal*, March 19, 2005.

19. Yochi J. Dreazen, Greg Ip, and Nicholas Kulish, "Big Business: Why the Sudden Rise In the Urge to Merge And Form Oligopolies?" *Wall Street Journal*, February 25, 2003.

20. "Pepsi, Ocean Spray Form Alliance," *AdWeek*, July 12, 2006.

21. Dan Campbell, "A Perfect Storm: Farmland Trustee Sues Ex-officers, Directors for 'Gross Negligence' in Co-ops Collapse," *Rural Cooperatives*, March–April 2005.

22. Suresh Persaud and Luther Tweeten, "Impact of Agribusiness Market Power on Farmers," chap. 7 in L. Tweeten and S. Thompson, eds., *Agricultural Policy for the 21st Century* (Iowa State Press, 2002).

23. Steve Hannaford, "Both Sides Now," *Harvard Business Review*, March 1, 2005.

24. Felicity Lawrence, John Vidal, and Steven Morris, "Unfair Trade Winds," *Guardian*, May 17, 2003.

25. For example, see "Companies Can Save up to 5% of Their Annual Purchasing Spend by Focusing on Key Suppliers," *Logistics Today*, August 2, 2005. Also "At Today's Cisco Systems, the Fewer Suppliers the Better," *Purchasing*, April 20, 2006.

26. See www.hildebrandt.com.

27. Ibid.

28. Jarred Schenke, "Law Firms Consider Mergers," *Atlanta Business Chronicle*, April 11, 2003.

29. As documented on the Web site of the International Legal Resource Group.

CHAPTER 3. GROW OR DIE

1. Wouter Dessein, Luis Garicano, and Robert H. Gertner, "Why Mergers Fail: Beyond Culture Clashes," *Capital Ideas*, December 2005.

2. Similar ideas are found at www.ideoplex.com.

3. The exceptions are small airline Morris Air (1999) and a piece of bankrupt ATA (2004).

4. "Hollywood Stores Drag Down Same-Store Earnings for Movie Gallery," *Portland Business Journal*, November 14, 2006.

5. Discussed in Robert F, Bruner, "All M&A Is Local," *The Batter Briefing*, 2004. Also Debra Crawford, "M&A: The Global Feeding Frenzy Continues," *Global Finance*, March 1998,

6. Khali Henderson "The Letter," *Phone Plus Magazine* online, December 2003.

7. "Overestimating merger synergies," *The McKinsey Quarterly Chart Focus Newsletter*, March 2005,

8. Gretchen Morgenson, "Sometimes Investors Should Just Say No," *New York Times*, August 14, 2005.

9. Ibid.

10. Gretchen Morgenson, "No Wonder CEOs Love Those Mergers," *New York Times*, July 18, 2004.

11. Ibid.

12. For those who are curious, a good description is at Philip E. Orbanes, "The Canasta Craze," www.thegamesjournal.com, August 2000.

13. That's the subject of Ted Nace, *Gangs of America* (Berrett-Koehler Publishers, 2003).

CHAPTER 4. DISRUPTION AND INNOVATION

1. Quaker was bought by PepsiCo in 2000, so Pepsi now sells Gatorade.

2. Carolyn Koo, "Nestlé to Buy PowerBar," TheStreet.com, February 23, 2002.

3. Carol Emert, "Nestlé SA Gobbles Up PowerBar," *San Francisco Chronicle*, February 24, 2000.

4. "Food Bars: A Small Package That's Leading to Large Profits," *Packaged Facts*, September 2003.

5. Tom Peters, *Reimagine: Business Excellence in a Disruptive Age!* (DK Adult, 2003).

6. Henry Mintzberg, *Managers Not MBAs* (Prentice Hall, 2004).

7. John P. Kotter, *Leading Change* (Harvard Business School Press, 1996).

8. Joseph Schumpeter, *Capitalism, Socialism, and Democracy*, 3rd ed. (New York: Harper and Brothers, orig. pub. 1942).

9. American efficiency expert (1856–1915), he popularized the term "scientific management." He also started the trend of standing over workers with a stopwatch. See Robert Kanigel, *The One Best Way: Frederick Winslow Taylor and the Enigma of Efficiency* (Penguin, 1999).

10. "The Top 100 Most Innovative Companies Ranking," *BusinessWeek*, April 24, 2006.

11. For example, see James Surowecki, "All Together Now," *New Yorker*, April 11, 2005.

12. G. Harris, "Where Are All The New Drugs?" *New York Times*, October 5, 2003.

13. Ibid.

14. Ibid.

15. Clayton M. Christensen, *The Innovator's Dilemma* (Harvard Business School Press, 1997).

16. Om Malik, "The New Road to Riches," *Business 2.0*, October 1, 2004.

17. David Hornik, www.ventureblog.com, October 24, 2005. Hornik is a partner of venture capital firm August Capital.

18. Adam Lashiunsky, "Turning Viral Videos into a Net Brand," *Fortune*, May 11, 2006.

19. Carole Resnick, "What We Need to Know About the Corporate Takeover of the 'Organic' Food Market," www.peacecouncil.net.

20. Carl Murphy, "The Green Business Revolution," *Fortune*, June 4, 2003.

21. Melanie Warner, "Wal-Mart Eyes Organic Foods," *New York Times*, March 12, 2006.

22. Ibid.

23. Bruno Cassiman, "The Impact of M&A on the R&D Process," August 2004, available at http://ideas.repec.org.

24. Former Vice Chairman of Lehman Brothers, his Peter J. Solomon Company has been an advisor on over 100 mergers, acquisitions, and company restructurings.

25. Quoted in Anna Muoio, "Is Bigger Better?" *Fast Company*, August 1998.

26. James E. Bessen and Michael J. Meurer, "The Patent Litigation Explosion," Boston University School of Law Working Paper no. 05-18, October 20, 2005.

27. According to the U.S. Patent and Trademark Office, Performance and Accountability Report for Fiscal 2005.

28. Jeffery A. Hellman, "All Buttoned Up," *Los Angeles Business Journal*, March 28, 2005.

29. As cited by Amit Asaravala, "Open Source Takes on Hardware Biz," *Wired*, June 17, 2003.

30. Available at www.alcatel.com.

31. *2005 Duke Law and Technology Review*, March 1, 2005.

32. Ibid.

33. Ibid.

34. Robert S. Boynton, "The Tyranny of Copyright," *New York Times* magazine, January 25, 2004.

35. Ibid.

36. Ibid.

CHAPTER 5. PRICES AND COSTS

1. The U.S. Bureau of Labor Statistics figures show consumer price index increases of less than 4 percent during every year between 1991 and 2004 (both 1990 and 2005 were somewhat higher).

2. As frequently pointed out throughout Charles Fishman, *The Wal-Mart Effect* (The Penguin Press, 2006).

3. Available at www.globalinsight.com. Global Insight was hired by Wal-Mart to do the study, so it might not be totally impartial. However, other studies cited seem to bear their estimates out.

4. There's a comprehensive set of charts of the history of oil prices available at www.wtrg.com/prices.htm.

5. Amey Stone, "CPI and Housing Prices," *BusinessWeek*, August 16, 2006.

6. Jane Bryant Quinn, "Cutting the Commissions," *Newsweek*, July 18, 2005.

7. National Coalition on Health Care, "Health Insurance Cost," www.nchc.org.

8. Daniel Gross, "Who Suffers From Inflation? It's not you. It's rich people," Slate.com, July 19, 2005, quoting Goldman Sachs economist Avinash Kaza.

9. Betsy Schiffman, "Kick Music Execs While They're Down," *Forbes*, October 1, 2002.

10. "Nine Face Charges Over NHS 'Price Cartel' Allegations," *The Guardian*, April 5, 2006.

11. David Usborne, "Former Heads of Top Auction Houses Charged with Price-Fixing," *The Independent*, March 3, 2001.

12. "Vitamin Makers Settle Vast Price Fixing Case," press release from the office of the New York State Attorney General, October 10, 2000.

13. Anthony Fletcher, "European Court Upholds Fines for Citric Acid Cartel," www.foodnavigator.com, September 28, 2005.

14. Statement before the U.S. Senate Subcommittee on Antitrust, Business Rights, and Competition, March 4, 1999.

15. Testimony of Deborah Platt Majoras to the U.S. Senate Committee on Commerce, Science, and Transportation and the Committee on Energy and Natural Resources, November 9, 2005.

16. Robert Milne and Jack E, Pace III, "Conspiratoligists at the Gate: The Scope of Expert Testimony on the Subject of Conspiracy in a Sherman Antitrust Case," *Antitrust* 2 (Spring 2003): 37.

17. Ibid.

18. Ibid.

19. Jonathan B. Baker, Director, Bureau of Economics, FTC, "Horizontal Price Fixing in Cyberspace," speech at 1996 conference, March 7, 1996.

20. Peter Coy, "A Pump Price Conspiracy?" *BusinessWeek*, September 6, 2006.

21. Nelson D. Schwartz, "Why Gas Prices Dropped," *Fortune*, October 16, 2006.

22. Barry C. Lynn, *End of the Line: The Rise and Coming Fall of the Global Corporation* (Doubleday, 2005).

23. Ibid., 22.

24. Ibid., 42.

25. For example, see Rhys Jenkins, "The Political Economy of Industrial Policy: Automobile Manufacture in the Newly Industrialising Countries," *Cambridge Journal of Economics* 19(5): 625–45.

26. Karen E. Klein, "Where's My Check?" *BusinessWeek*, October 16, 2005.

27. Notably in Fishman, *The Wal-Mart Effect*, 79.

28. Marian Kester Coombs, "The High Cost of Low Prices," *The American Conservative*, May 22, 2006, a review of the Fishman book.

29. Fishman, *The Wal-Mart Effect*, 82.

30. "Tyson Loses Cattle-Price Lawsuit," *Wall Street Journal*, February 17, 2004.

31. Samira Jafari, "Ranchers Must Pay Tyson's Expenses in Cattle Case," Associated Press, August 26, 2005.

32. Organization for Competitive Markets, *OCM Newsletter*, March 2002.

33. Fishman, *The Wal-Mart Effect*, 94.

34. Paul Krugman, "Enron's Biggest Losers: Employees," *Wall Street Journal*, December 5, 2001.

35. Jacob Hacker, *The Great Risk Shift* (Oxford University Press, 2006), 66.

36. Jed Greer and Kavaljit Singh, "A Brief History of Transnational Corporations," www.globalpolicy.org, 2000.

37. Adrian Michaels, "Swatch Says It Did Not Violate Laws," *Financial Times*, August 12, 2004.

38. Timothy Aeppel, "Why Dollar Can't Close Gap," *Wall Street Journal*, March 23, 2005.

CHAPTER 6. OLIGOPOLIES AND PUBLIC POLICY

1. Jeffrey H. Birnbaum, "The Road to Riches Is Called K Street," *Washington Post*, June 22, 2005.

2. Jeffrey H. Birnbaum, "Lobbying Here to Stay Despite Scandal," *San Jose Mercury News*, September 17, 2006.

3. Ibid.

4. Jeffrey H. Birnbaum, "Clients' Rewards Keep K Street Lobbyists Thriving," *Washington Post*, February 14, 2006.

5. Jean Cummings, "Cautiously, Starbucks Puts Lobbying on Corporate Menu," *Wall Street Journal*, April 12, 2005.

6. Clay Risen, "Store Lobby," *New Republic*, July 25, 2005.

7. Alden and Neil Buckley, "Wal-Mart Becomes Largest Corporate Political Investor," *Financial Times*, February 24, 2004.

8. Jeanne Cummings, "Wal-Mart Opens for Business in Tough Market: Washington," *Wall Street Journal*, March 24, 2005.

9. Dean Starkman, "Cities Use Eminent Domain To Clear Lots For Big-Box Stores," *Wall Street Journal*, December 8, 2004.

10. Ibid.

11. Kortney Stringer, "Wal-Mart's Surge Leaves Dead Stores Behind," *Wall Street Journal*, September 9, 2004.

12. Parija Bhatnagar, "Eminent Domain: A Big Box Bonanza?" CNNmoney.com, June 24, 2005.

13. Joshua Kurlantzick, "Condemnation Nation: Retail Chains and the Big Business of Eminent Domain," *Harper's Magazine*, October 2005.

14. Julia Virtullo-Martin, "Thinking about Eminent Domain," *Center for Rethinking Development Newsletter*, February 2005.

15. Natalie Kosteini, "Debate over KOZ Coming to a Boil," *Philadelphia Business Journal*, June 7, 2004.

16. Andrew Cassel, "If Comcast Can Afford Disney, It Can Pay State, Local Taxes," *Philadelphia Inquirer*, February 18, 2004. At the time, it seemed as if cable giant Comcast was about to acquire Disney.

17. "Norway Lenders Back Kvaerner Plan," *New York Times*, January 4, 2002.

18. "CIGNA to Stay in Philadelphia, Not Move to N.J.," *Insurance Journal*, April 27, 2004.

19. Cassel, "If Comcast Can Afford Disney."

20. James Wallace, "Boeing: Tax Breaks No Bargaining Chip," *Seattle Post-Intelligencer*, October 29, 2004.

21. Stanley Holmes, "Behind Boeing's Sweet 7e7 Deal," March 26, 2004.

22. Chris Koepfer, "Let the Bidding Begin," *Production Machining*, July 2006.

23. Anne Marie Squeo and J. Lynn Lunsford, "How Two Officials Got Caught By Pentagon's Revolving Door," *Wall Street Journal*, December 18, 2003.

24. Ibid.

25. Anne Marie Squeo, "Mergers Make It Tougher to Punish Federal Contractors," *Wall Street Journal*, June 10, 2003.

26. "Pension Pork," *The Economist*, April 17, 2004.

27. David C. John, "Final Pension Agreement Places Corporate Interests above Taxpayer Interests," www.heritage.org, April 16, 2004.

28. Neil King Jr., "Salesmen for America," *Wall Street Journal*, May 2006. Also Neil King Jr., "U.S. Rallies Companies to Play Role in Diplomacy," *Wall Street Journal*, February 17, 2006.

29. Neil King Jr., "Goodwill Hunting," *Wall Street Journal*, February 17, 2006.

30. Laura Eggerton, "Giant Food Companies Control Standards," *Toronto Star*, April 28, 1999.

31. Ibid.

32. Diane Farsetta, "The Cows Have Come Home," CorpWatch.com, September 1, 2005.

33. Elizabeth Drew, "Selling Washington," *New York Review of Books*, June 23, 2005.

34. Melody Peterson, "Making Drugs, Shaping the Rules," *New York Times*, February 1, 2004.

35. Ibid.

36. Marcy Gordon, "KPMG Probes Ex-partners Unlawful Conduct," Associated Press, June 16, 2005.

CHAPTER 7. CONVERGENCE, CHOICE, AND CONSOLIDATION

1. Stephen Richter, "J'accuse—It's Always the Others' Fault—Daimler-Chrysler Merger," *Chief Executive*, February 2001.

2. "The Great English Divide," *BusinessWeek*, August 13, 2001.

3. Yadong Luo and Oded Shenkar, "The Multinational Corporation as a Multilingual Community: Language and Organization in a Global Context," *Journal of International Business* Studies (2006) 37, 321–39.

4. Jerry Useem, "The Winner-Steal-All Society and the Persistence of the CEO-Market Myth," *American Prospect*, October 21, 2002.

5. Idea inspired by Patrick Gerard, author of the Web site "Performance and Reward," which has some astute things to say about executive compensation.

6. Al Gore, according to David Gergen, *Eyewitness to Power* (Touchstone Books, October 2001), chap. 9.

7. Sarah Ellison and Deborah Ball, "Food companies hunt for the next big diet fad," *Wall Street Journal*, February 16, 2006.

8. Tara Siegel Bernard, "The More the Merrier: One Franchise Mantra," *Wall Street Journal*, January 13, 2004.

9. Edward Jay Epstein, *The Big Picture* (Random House, 2005), 17.

10. Federal Trade Commission and the U.S. Department of Justice, *Antitrust Guidelines for Collaborations Among Competitors*, April 2000, available at www.ftc.gov.

11. John R. Wilke, "Top Modeling Agencies Face Price-Fixing Inquiry," *Wall Street Journal*, August 3, 2003.

12. Ibid.

13. Gary Gentile, "Miramax Shines, Yet Fate Teeters," Associated Press, January 5, 2001.

14. "The Organic Myth," *BusinessWeek*, October 15, 2006.

15. Anderson, *The Long Tail* (Hyperion, 2006), 18.

16. Wikipedia has an article on "Duff Beer."

17. Tom Bux, "Time to Dump the 'Low Carb' Beers," *Blogcritics Magazine*, blogcritics.org, November 23, 2003.

18. Suzette Hackney, "Loyal to the King: Imported Beer Isn't Welcome in Bud's Home," *Detroit Free Press*, October 26, 2006.

19. See www.internettime.com/blog.

20. Barry Schwartz, *The Paradox of Choice* (Ecco/HarperCollins, 2004) 29.

21. Ibid.

22. As convincingly described in Naomi Klein, *No Logo: Taking Aim at the Brand Bullies* (Picador, 2000).

23. John Carvel, "Retail Chains 'Cloning' UK Towns: Global Brands Are Swamping the Individuality of the High Streets," *The Guardian*, June 6, 2005.

24. Ibid.

CHAPTER 8. MARKET DOMINATION IN THREE INDUSTRIES

1. Anthony Fletcher, "Still Drinks Market Growing Faster Than Carbonates," BeverageDaily.com, September 2, 2006.

2. The term was made famous in a 1980 book by J.C. Louis and Harvey Z. Yazijian, *The Cola Wars: The Story of the Global Battle between the Coca-Cola Company and PepsiCo, Inc.* (Everest House, 1980).

3. Marc Kaufman, "Fighting the Cola Wars in Schools," *Washington Post*, March 23, 1999.

4. "Soft Drinks Are Hot—and Getting Hotter," Beverage Daily News.com, December 16, 2003.

5. Melanie Warner, "In America, Soda Sales Are Losing Their Sparkle," *International Herald Tribune*, March 3, 2006. Reporting on a *Beverage Digest* study.

6. "UK Soft Drinks Market: Carbonates Losing Their Sparkle," *Drinks Business Review*, March 21, 2006, See also Warner, "In America."

7. Jack Ewing, "A Cold Shoulder For Coca-Cola in Germany," *BusinessWeek*, May 2, 2005.

8. National Soft Drink Association (renamed the American Beverage Association in 2004) white paper, "Growing Up Together: The Soft Drink Industry and America."

9. From *Beverage Age*, February 2001.

10. William A. Roberts, Jr., "New Products Conference Report: A True Desert Adventure." *Prepared Foods*, December 11, 2003.

11. Steve Holtz, "Quality, Not Quantity," *CSP Magazine*, March 4, 2004.

12. "Bottled Water Continued Tradition of Strong Growth in 2005," press release, Beverage Marketing Corporation, April 2006.

13. Lee Clifford, "Winning in the Water Fight," *Fortune*, March 4, 2002.

14. John G. Rodwan, Jr., "Bottled Water 2004: U.S. and International Statistics and Developments," *Bottled Water Reporter*, April–May 2005.

15. John G. Rodwan, Jr., "Bottled Water 2005," *Water Conditioning and Purification Magazine*, September 2006.

16. John Lofstock, "What's Selling: A View From the Customers: Part II," *Convenience Store Decisions*, November 4, 2006.

17. Betsy McKay, "Pepsi, Coke Take Opposite Tacks In Bottled Water Marketing Battle," *Wall Street Journal*, April 18, 2002.

18. "Coca-Cola Alters Delivery System for Wal-Mart; Bottlers Sue," *Birmingham Business Journal*, February 14, 2006.

19. Edward Jay Epstein, *The Big Picture*, 203.

20. Harvey Feigenbaum, "Hollywood: The Bottom Line." *Le monde diplomatique*, August 2005.

21. Based on an analysis of figures at BoxOfficeMojo.com.

22. Speech by Dan Glickman, president and CEO of the Motion Picture Association of America, March 15, 2005.

23. Arthur De Vany and Henry McMillan, "Was the Antitrust Action That Broke Up the Movie Studios Good for the Movies? Evidence from the Stock Market," *American Law and Economics Review* 6(1): 135–53.

24. See www.boxofficemojo.com.

25. Bruce Weber, "Liked the Movie, Loved the Megaplex," *New York Times*, August 17, 2005.

26. Dan Ackman, "Movie Theaters of the Absurd," *Forbes*, March 1, 2001.

27. Warren Gump, "Stadium Theaters = Massive Losses," Motley Fool, July 13, 2000. Also Kristina Stefanova, "Overexposed—Too Many Movie Theaters Leads to Failure," *Insight on the News*, December 18, 2000.

28. Dan Ackman, "Disaster of the Day: Movie Theaters," *Forbes*, January 23, 2001.

29. Russ Banham, "The Phantom of the Megaplex," *CFO Magazine*, January 1, 2001.

30. Jeff Tyson, "How Movie Distribution Works," hostuffworks.com (explains the precise mathematics).

31. "AMC and Loews to Merge as Consolidation Continues," *Los Angeles Times*, June 2, 2005.

32. Edward Jay Epstein, "The Popcorn Palace Economy," Slate.com. January 2, 2006.

33. Alex Markels, "A Movie Theater Revival, Aided by Teenagers," *New York Times, August 2, 2003*.

34. Jane L. Levere, "Advertisers Pour More Money Into the Big Screen," *New York Times*, June 27, 2005.

35. Laura Petrecca and David Lieberman, "Film Fans Can Expect More Advertising on Big Screen," *USA Today*, December 6, 2005.

36. Epstein, "Popcorn Palace."

37. Based on an analysis of figures in boxofficemojo.com.

38. Michael Sragow, "Swatting away Fabricated Buzz with Genuine Word of Mouth," *Baltimore Sun*, November 3, 2006.

39. A. O. Scott, " 'Pirates of the Caribbean': Eat My Jetsam," *New York Times*, July 7, 2006.

40. Epstein, *The Big Picture*, 341.

41. Based on a report from Levin & Associates, a consulting firm that also produces the *Health Care M & A Monthly Newsletter*.

42. M. Asif Ismail, "Drug Lobby Second to None: How the Pharmaceutical Industry Gets Its Way in Washington," The Center for Public Integrity, July 7. 2005.

43. Diedtra Henderson, "Backed by Study, Pfizer Intensifies Lipitor Pitch," *Boston Globe*, September 5, 2006.

44. Figures from IMS Health and "The Statin Drugs: Prescriptions and Price Trends," Consumers Union, January 2006.

45. Consumers Union, 2.

46. John Simons, "The $10 Billion Pill. Hold the Fries, Please. Lipitor, the Cholesterol-Lowering Drug, Has Become the Bestselling Pharmaceutical in History. Here's How Pfizer Did It," *Fortune*, January 20, 2003.

47. "Aventis: Investors Await Their Award," *BusinessWeek*, February 2, 2004.

48. See company Web site www.bms.com.

49. Peter Benesh, "Big Drug Companies Keep Getting Better," *Investor's Business Daily*, October 27, 2006.

50. Emilie Reymond, "Big Pharma Splash Out on R&D," Drugrearcher.com, October 24, 2006.

51. Amy Barrett, "Pfizer's Funk," *BusinessWeek*, February 28, 2005.

52. " 'Generic Drugs Are Experiencing Faster Sales Growth Than Many Branded Ones, and This Trend Is Set to Continue,' Says visiongain," BusinessWire, November 17, 2005. Also Brian Lawler, "The Coming Generic Drug Boom," Motley Fool (fool.com), October 16, 2006.

53. From visiongain report, "The World's Top Ten Generic Companies 2005," as reported on BusinessWire, November 17, 2005.

54. "2005 US Sales of Generic Prescription Drugs Could Exceed $28B," *Pharma Industry News*, September 21, 2006.

55. Marianne Barium, "Bulking Up in the Drugs Industry," *The Guardian*, September 26, 2006.

56. According to George Barrett, Teva North America CEO, in Senate hearing testimony, July 25, 2006.

57. As noted in Tom Branna, "A Pause in the Growth of Generics?" *Pharma and Bio Ingredients*, July 2006.

58. The two companies, originally one, were separated during the First World War.

59. Meir P. Pugatch, "Big Pharma Strikes Back," *Pharmaceutical Executive Europe*, September 1, 2006.

60. "Medco to Pay $155 Million in Kickback Case," *New York Times*, October 24, 2006.

61. Claimed on Medco Web site at phx.corporate-ir.net.

62. Milt Freudenheim, "In Switch, Insurer Lets Stores Fill 90-Day Prescriptions," *New York Times*, April 15, 2005.

63. Matthew Boyle, "Drug Wars," CNNmoney.com, June 13, 2005.

64. Michael Cecil, "A Drug-Price Avalanche?" Motley Fool, September 27, 2006.

CONCLUSION

1. Available at www.antitrustreview.com/archives/631.

2. William H. Page, "The Ideological Origins and Evolution of Antitrust Law," in *Issues in Competition Law and Policy*, ed. Wayne Dale Collins (ABA Antitrust Section, forthcoming).

3. Available at www.antitrustreview.com/archives/631.

Index

About the Author

STEPHEN G. HANNAFORD is a consultant and writer, specializing in the interaction between technology and business. Since 2003, he has served as editor and publisher of Oligopoly Watch, a market watchdog site; he is also executive editor at Progressive Business Publications, overseeing the series *Better Buys for Business*. He is the author or co-author of several books, including *Workflow Reengineering* and *Teams and the Graphic Arts Service Provider*, and he regularly speaks to industry and professional groups on issues of technology and business.